IT HAS TO DO WITH SEEING

THE COLLECTED POEMS
OF
MOIRA BAILIS

VOLUME II

DAVID MESSINEO, EDITOR
MELANIE A. PIMONT, ASSISTANT EDITOR

The Poet's
Press

PITTSBURGH, PA

This is the 191st publication of
THE POET'S PRESS
2209 Murray Avenue #3
Pittsburgh, PA 15217
www.poetspress.org

This book is also published as a PDF Ebook.

ISBN 0-922558-54-X (paperback)
ISBN 0-92258-55-8 (hardcover)

TABLE OF CONTENTS

NATURE

DAY TURNS TO NIGHT

THE CONSPIRACY OF SEASONS

VARIATIONS ON A THEME

CLOSING REMARKS

NOTES

Childhood

News of Uisneach

I feel a rush of nostalgia
reading your letter
written on a breezy day
in Ireland.

You write
"the crows are tumbling
over the hill of Uisneach"
that place sacred
in ancient times.

I am carried away
to the boglands
of my Westmeath birthplace,
hear the endless cawing
of crows in the woods
around my home.

Flying home in the evening
to the ruined tower near my home,
they were black flags
unfurled in the greying sky,
their harsh cawing
unforgotten with age.

<3>

The Hour of My Birth

The hour of my birth
was in the dark dawn
of a February morning.
My mother labored
to bring me forth
to partake of life
and all its joys and sorrows.

The river flowed past our house.
At that great moment of my coming
the dogs howled in the passageway
the sound mingled with my mother's tears.
I arrived as the dawn
streaked the sky with red.

The sound of wind in the trees
waited for me,
the translucent sky
the songs of birds
and the scent of roses
was held for me in Time's hollow hand.

I entered the valley of life
but my eyes were always on the stars.
Sadness and joy awaited me —
and the scent of roses.
Love and friendship awaited me
and passion, red like a drop of blood.

<4>

Nineteen Twenty-One

Nineteen twenty-one
was my year
the year I chose to come

All the generations waited
for me
It was the year of storms
the countryside blazed
and gunshots rammed
the silence of the woods
the year
my mother's agony began

<5>

A House with No Key

We live, each within a house
built of our pasts,
a house with no key, only
memory.
These days, I find myself
describing memories
but hardly sharing them.

"Yes, I know Connemara.
I went there as a child.
I was five years old
when I saw them
pulling my brother from
the Atlantic.
I remember the waves
roaring in on the gray strand
and a sound like birds crying
as they carried my soaking
brother to safety."

But this telling is only
as meaningful as a snapshot
explained,
a finger pointing
to the soft, sweet faces
of the children in Connemara
in a faded photograph.

<6>

The listeners can express
sympathy, amazement,
wonder. There is no way they can
hear the wind from the sea,
the cries of the women,
the sobs of the near-drowned boy,
or know the terror felt
by the child who stood by
who watched
and remembered.

Sometimes

Sometimes I imagine
I put the key in the door
walk into the narrow hall
and step into the pretty
room with its big windows
and she's there
sitting by the fire
and she smiles
as she did the day
I woke her from sleep
in that same chair
and her smile was as
warm and welcoming
as a sparkling fire
on a winter day

<8>

The Journey

In the cave of leafiness
I'm standing
five years old
distant humming
that unselfconscious
life humming away
and I am listening
to this primordial sound
I do not yet know
our curse — to know
to be aware — to
always care —
innocent unknowing
the ungraspable secret
pulsing life
somehow knowing there
is a continuum
a secret world we cannot
enter — like childhood

I could not find them
the answer to the secretive
sound
I cannot now find
answers to the longing
of my heart
This inverse awareness
stays with me
like a wound exposed
to air the pain of
awareness — knowing
not knowing
sweet
felt sweet sadness

<9>

Demesne

This was at the beginning
when the leaf on the trees
was a tender green
and the buds reached
to the sun.
In the shrubbery
the faint hum of bees,
the ache of melancholy
a longing that could not be satisfied,
unbidden, a welling up of tears,
for what . . .

In the lost demesne
the river ran slow and deep
and the trees sighed in the wind.
The bees did not question
their fate, just did
what had to be done.
The ache foretold love
and loss.
Neither one exists
without the other.

All the humming of the bees
cannot shake
the awfulness of perception.
The enemy hides within
the gates —
if all is well
it is an illusion
a dream image
feeling nowhere
leads into truth.
Truth is the work of the bees.

<10>

Down the highway
waiting in the shadows
something wails
shrouded
head bowed
waiting.

<11>

The Lost Wood

Near the stony hills, the wood,
hidden on an old demesne was mine.
Not through endowment
but through love, I made it so.

It was lovely.
Murmuring pigeons lulled the days,
bees hummed in the hedges.
A child's enchanted playground —
remembering moves me to tears.

The seasons were canticles.
The whins, glorious in autumn,
gold cups sanctified by the sun,
their musky scent like sachets
in an old dresser.

Stormy winter nights, moonlight
flooded the aisles of trees.
It was magic there.
A fox barked at the moon,
the elms roared
in a bitter wind.

In the joyful spring, violets
an enchantment on the grass
a blue shawl misting the glades.
The flutes of birdsong chorused
in the galleries of trees
in the greening glades.

<12>

Fifty years ago, a wartime spring
the wood was cut for timber.
The fox homeless, pigeons routed,
the scent of whins and violets
blown on the wind, forever lost.
My sanctuary gone.
My wood only a memory
of centuries of song.

<13>

Path

For each of us then is a
scrap piece of earth more dear
than any other.

Down that path I go in
memory
bordered by whins,
their gold cups raised
to the autumn sun,
their musky smell
scenting the air,
their shadowed aisles
hiding the lair
of the secretive fox.
How I long again for
the solace of your
companionable trees
and the hedges filled
with the murmur of trees
and the wild rose
pink petals.

<14>

Proper Manners

I saw a teapot.
Sprays of wildflowers
on its rotund sides,
a gold knob on the lid.
Coated with a creamy glaze
it speaks to me
of gentility.

I recall
mother's tea parties
long ago in Ireland.
The proverbial
cucumber sandwiches,
iced coffee cake,
the best china.

A bevy of ladies
in flowered hats,
graceful tea gowns.
A flow of small talk,
light and lilting tones.
The essence
of propriety,

and myself, six years old,
sitting quietly in
an upright chair, hands
folded in my lap,
saying nothing.
Which is why, years later,
I remember everything.

This poem was later revised and retitled "Company Manners."
That revision was alternately titled "Tea Party."

<15>

Company Manners

Dublin, 1927

Today I saw a teapot,
sprays of wildflowers
on its rotund sides,
a plump knob on its lid.
Coated with a creamy glaze,
it speaks to me of gentility.

Seeing it reminds me of
my mother's tea parties
long ago, in Ireland:
wreathed in roses,
our best china plates
neatly laid beside
napkins, gauze-thin;
our lace-edged tablecloth
starched to perfection.

A silver sugar bowl
sits beside a milk jug.
On silver dishes lay
iced coffee cake;
the cucumber sandwiches
quintessential.

My mother's friends,
a bevy of ladies
in flowered hats,
in flowing tea-gowns,
inconsequentially chatter
in light and lilting tones,
their flow of sweet talk
the essence of propriety.

<16>

And myself, six years old,
sitting quietly in
an upright chair, hands
folded in my lap,
saying nothing.
Which is why, years later,
I remember everything.

*The version of "Company Manners" above is a new revision
that includes recently rediscovered edits in Moira's
handwriting, penned sometime after 2003, to modify the
version that was published in her 2003 chapbook* poems.

<17>

Ciotóg

When I was ten my mother
tried to teach me how to sew,
gave me a square of pink linen,
said, "Take this needle and thread
and I'll show you
how it goes."

So every afternoon we sat
companionably.
I watched my mother sewing,
the needle stitching through
the patterned cloth
in her right hand,
making a summer dress
long ago in Ireland.

"Show me," I asked, "show me
how to sew." She gave me
a square of linen —
"That'll be a handkerchief," she said,
and handed me a needle and thread.

Watching my mother I rolled a hem
then tried to follow the movements of her hand.
"I can't do it," I said, in tears.

Laughing, she took the needle
and the cloth, reversed direction, said
"Use your right hand, dearest,
you're not ciotóg."[1]

---

[1] *Ciotóg.* Gaelic. A left-handed person.

<18>

Money

When I was a child
at the local school in Ireland
my math teacher taught us practical
things for when, said she,
"You are grown up."

Her class on the use of money
was one we enjoyed.
She taught us the use of money
and the names of coins:
pounds, shillings, pence.

One day my brother,
sitting at the dinner table,
was impatient. He banged his hands
together to get attention.
My father reprimanded —
"James, stop pounding your hands."
I listened, confused —
where was the money in this?

<19>

Disappointments of Childhood

You told me how
On that long ago day
Your mother dressed you
Warm as a teddy bear
To go with Daddy
To the Dublin Zoo.

Your mother said "you"
will see the monkeys
and the elephant
and lions in big cages.

But, you said, through tears,
Daddy changed his plan.
"It's going to rain," he said.
The plan was canceled.

It's been ages since that day
but she recalled
looking back years and years.

<20>

Jamestown 1928 (Early Version)

One afternoon in summer
years ago
my childish slow footsteps
followed you
through the old garden
rain-soaked from
early showers
glowing with berries
and summer blossoms
to where the Shannon
quietly flowed.

This was your paradise
the house, two hundred years
surrounded by woods
then, in that silent world
the only sound the trees.

<21>

Jamestown 1928

I remember Jamestown
that summer of 1928.
I followed you
through the summer berries
that led to the secret recesses
of the garden
to where the Shannon River,
haunt of herons,
slowly flowed.

Tall trees cast summer shadows
on the rough grass in the meadow.
High vowels of the wind
sounded through, and
scatters of rain,
handfuls of water,
blew in my face.

Last year I stopped by the gates
fallen crookedly from their stone posts.
There was a kind of sighing
in the leaves of the few oaks
left standing by the avenue.

What is there about lost places
haunted by scenes of childhood?
All the land built over
and the house gone,
the only vestige of the old place

<22>

a broken wall, a space
where the house stood,
as though the future
was a giant crevasse
that opened up
and swallowed forever
the child's paradise.

The sun is
always shining
in the past.

<23>

Summer 1935

> Photo on tennis court
> Sun going down
> Shadows will lie
> Cover them

<24>

Dalkey

I remember Dalkey.
One afternoon in summer
Years ago,
The train drew into
Its small Victorian station.
You were waiting there.
You kissed my hand.
How chivalrous you were.

We walked away
Up the steep road
To the little castle
On the hill
Above the bay.

Sitting on the scented grass
We talked of what
Had come to pass.
I was only seventeen.
I cried but knew
The someone I had sought
Just was not you.

I remember now
The hurt in your eyes.
I hardly said good-bye.
Knowing this a grief
I could not share,
I left you there.

A lark soared
Into the blue air,
Its song a threnody.
I listened and sighed.
How does one mourn
A love that bloomed
And died?

<25>

Merdon

How mysterious is memory and the gift of recall!
The poet, when he saw the little ball
Balanced on a jet of water in a window
Remembered a time and place from long ago;
I recall a place I used to know,
Part of my being and my very soul.

Some March days then, a soft wind
Blew from the south and carried on the air.
The scent of pine forests in the Wicklow hills,
The promise of soft weather unfulfilled
As once again the east winds blustered in the trees.

Then came the fierce equinoctial gales
And the rain lashed window panes
Reflected broken light from the stormy sky,
The hills echoed a seabird's lonely cry,
And snowdrops showed their chilly faces by the
hedge.

In summers in the sparkling air,
daisies starred the meadow grass,
swifts swooped and swerved about the ivied eaves
pink roses and the leaves
of lilac, laburnum and fuchsia were tender
        in the sunlight.

On warm August nights a full
And silver moon whitened the castle on the hill,
In the meadow behind the granite wall
We heard the corncrake's steady call
And saw the shadows of the pine trees on the court.

Autumn, purple asters graced the flower beds
And bronze chrysanthemums and Michelmas daisies.
Mornings we gathered mushrooms
        on the dew-drenched hill.
The last tomatoes ripened on the window sill.
The tang of burning leaves was on the air.

<26>

Wild geese flew southward under a hunter's moon
A chill came in the rooms
That foretold winter and the passing days.
Early coal fires flickered in the grates.
Evening light died sadly down the sky.

In winter's chill, under a wan sun
The pine trees swayed in a cold north wind;
On frosty days I recall the rimed grass
And my father tapped the old glass
In the dark hallway and forecast a shower of hail.

The spumy Irish Sea raced in the bay,
Grey waves crashed against the grey sea wall,
The lamps were haloed with rings of misty light,
Foghorns warned all through the night
And wind in the chimney made a lonesome
        wailing sound.

Now I recall the slow and stately days
Part of my being and my very soul,
The passing of the seasons long ago,
Thoughts of the places that I used to know,
Come to me now in sadness and in joy.

<27>

The Porch at Merdon[2]

The porch, whose doors face the west,
has large windows. The sun warms it well.
From here you can see north, south, east, and west,
forests and rivers, fields and tree-lined lanes.

When the oaks array themselves in green
and the linden's shade reaches the flower bed
the world disappears behind the blue bark
engraved by leaves into motley patches.

Here, at a tiny table, brother and sister
kneel, drawing scenes of battle and pursuit
and with their pink tongues try to help
great warships, one of which is smiling.

---

[2] *Merdon.* Name of the poet's parents' house in Dalkey. A very large brick house
built by a sea captain in 1887.

<28>

Neighborhood

All the homes were separated
by high walls, brick and cement.
Fancy iron gates opened to tidy yards.
We knew the neighbors' names
but rarely met them.

The walls, all five feet high
kept us separate from one another.
The roofs, rising above the trees,
hid the summer sky.
In the winter it didn't matter.

When we met on the foot path
we nodded a greeting.
Only the children spoke their names
to one another.
Only the children had hopes
for future friendships.

<29>

Cleaboy[3]

I
She stands on the graveled driveway —
This is her domain —
Overhead a plane drones —
flying somewhere
She is oblivious of that
the far-flung world
spliced by a network of routes.
She is rooted here
among the old beeches
at Cleaboy.

Today in the silence
the wild cawing of rooks
matches her mood.
A world is ending here —
this fenced-in realm
hedged fields
ditches filled.
Here she watched the slow
progress of the seasons,
listened to the winter winds
roaring in the copse.

II
In the summer's meadow
the slow progress of mares
feeding on the lush grass —
Now, all to end
as evanescent as any
dream world.
Soon only memories
or disturbing dreams —

---

[3] A family drama. The poem describes the poet's first cousin, Margaret Moore Clarke, who lost her extensive property — a stud farm named "Cleaboy" — to her daughter-in-law. This occurred after her son died of malarial encephalitis in Africa. Margaret, heart-broken, didn't live long after that.

<30>

"It was"
"I was here"
"It was mine"

The loss of a beloved place
as grievous
as the loss of a dear friend.
No longer sustained
we suffer
because each ending
reminds us of our own.
Her gaze follows the rolling fields
to the horizon — to
the bare winter trees.
The sound cries of the rooks
repeat.

III
To lose what one loves
a wrenching away
from the familiar
in swift progression —
trees, flowers, summer grasses
the gnarled branches of fruit trees
espaliered against a garden wall
comes before her eyes —
rook feathers among autumn leaves
the horses, images as in slow motion
cropping the meadow fields.
A home is a carapace,
a carapace torn away.

<31>

1944. Dublin

The Glen was really no more than a
cleft among the mountains, which
crowded up around it, making of it a
peaceful, quiet place, secluded from
the noisy world. There was
only one way of entering the glen, by
a sandy path, which ran through
thick woodland and wound above
the lake, long and dark, and, on sunless
days, somewhat sinister. The steep
slopes rising from the lake-sides
were covered with sturdy pine and fir
trees, their bright and dark green
needles a perfect setting for the
lake's silky blackness.
At the head of the lake, where the
grassy banks gave way to a sandy
curve of beach, stood a square, stone
house, its long old-fashioned windows
reflecting the rippling water and
waving pine branches. At one time,
nearly forty years before, the house
and lake and lands for miles around
were under one ownership, but times —

<32>

The Woman I Was Then

The woman I was then
is no longer me —
But I was once that
woman —
a naif —
yet crucified by an
awareness
of life, terror and
beauty —

<33>

The Darkness of a Cinema Long Ago

the darkness of a cinema
long ago —
he who gave it to my
mother was swept away
in the cataclysm of the
first World War —
it is as if these little
losses were
mementos
aids to memory — they
were more with me
when I could lift the
gold orange glass to the
light — fondle the pendant
as it hung from my neck on
its thin silver chain
and where has the green
and yellow bowl from Mespil
vanished to? It stood on my
window filled with that most
poignant flower — lily of the valley.
I am not reconciled
to the loss of little things
the gold bowl my father
gave me,
won for me — I was
seven years old
greater the loss
because, with one
heedless — careless sweep
of my arm — I knocked
it to the floor — its
hundred pieces irreparable
shattered

<34>

I am not reconciled
to the loss of the locket
lost in a cinema
they are woven into the
fabric of an unrecoverable
past
something of memory
perished with their loss

<35>

Feathers

You used to send me
feathers
sealed in
book markers
the wings of Irish birds
found while you
walked the wood
on Killiney Hill

<36>

All That Remain

The urns, hidden in the
undergrowth
are all that remain
of the past
down a tunnel into
the sunny days
sitting on the steps
the pigeons *coo coo coo*
and beyond the trees
the deep canal near
the old mill
and the winding road
to the bog land layer
and layer

<37>

Dreamwalking

Pale sunlight floods the hills,
Strikes sparks from the granite —
It is silent — only the gulls
Call and shimmer in a high, blue sky.
I know this lonely place —
Beloved in childhood,
These three hills lying
Between Dalkey and Killiney,
by the Irish Sea.

I wander through the pines —
The air smells fragrant, spicy.
At the old stone wall
Above the rocky quarries —
Blackberry and valerian bloom.
The scented yellow gorse stabs the air.
I hear the distant waves
Breaking on the far sea shore.

A sound in the woods
My heart reverberates —
Voices from the past,
Are calling, calling —
I will see them again,
The long-gone loved ones.
I turn towards the woods —
My feet move heavily —
No distance covered,
The light is fading —
The voices are silent.
Mist rises from the valley,
All turns evanescent —

<38>

Hills, woods, mountains —
All eddying and billowing
In a rushing stream of silver-blue light.
I am caught in a whirlwind —
I am falling, falling —
My cries unheeded, my arms outstretched
Through the soft darkness
And a roaring wind.

<39>

family and friends

Ancestor of Mine

An ancestor of mine
is buried on the banks
of the Wisconsin River.

I was there in September
and the boys were playing football
in the hazy autumn sunshine.

*A more detailed poem about this ancestor appears in the
"Variations on a Theme" section of this volume.*

<43>

Gertie — Wedding Day[1]

Last year I stood
by the granite wall
ivy-covered
In 1920 Spring you were
there my
navy suit and shell-pink
blouse and a navy hat
with a pink rose on its brim
and you smiled at the
camera

It was a pleasing day
post-war simplicity
in the hills the
guns sounded
the death knell of the old
regime
I was yet to come

Hand on his arm gentle
smiling faces look out at me
down 70 years
the family gathered
around that Spring day
April 1920

---

[1] This poem describes the marriage of the poet's mother, Gertrude Higgins, to
Andrew Moore. The reception was held in Longford.

<44>

Personal

Sometimes I walk to the cemetery.
My hair tousled by the wind.
I have sturdy legs.
Since I came here to dream
I've longed for a wooden seat
so I could gaze at the valley.

I'd like some time with children
where I could have fun.
It ain't the money — money ain't everything.
Look at Mother Teresa.

In the cold weather I wrap up.
Totally snuggled up I read alone at night.
I'm in awe of the moon's white face
outside my window.
I'd like to live in the country.
I've had my share of success —

Long ago grandfather died.
No one says his name now.
His name was simple, John.
Now I'm older than he was then.

<45>

Grandmother Moore

Conversation had a confidentiality,
sometimes lasted half an hour.
Someone's joys and another's miseries
were debated in low tones —
all the local news
and the parish priest passed by
greeting all the locals.
Caps were tipped and
the women smiled.

Once home she brewed some tea
and settled down to read
the daily papers —
"Just to see," she'd say,
"how things are going
far away."
Local news and event happenings
caught her attention.

She cooked her meals
and ate them, punctually.
A book propped up before her,
She'd turn the radio on —
in those days, only the BBC.

"Did you hear about" —
and in a low voice
a name would be pronounced
and sometimes, someone's shame,
his latest news discussed.

In those days little carts
came in from the country
pulled by donkeys.

<46>

As Grandmother walked in her leisurely way
from shop to shop she'd say
"Fine day" or "Please God
the rain will hold off today."

She knew the names
of all the owners
of the little shops where goods
were on display.
All she bought was written up
in a black book.

This was her unvarying routine —
for years, it seemed,
left her house at ten o'clock,
this lining up of news
sustained her through the quiet day.

This is the way
the days and months passed
in a small town on
the River Shannon
in Ireland, long ago.

<47>

A Simple Life

My grandmother led a simple life.
Each morning, after breakfast,
she walked down the quiet street
to the gray stone church —
to gain a benediction, she said.

On the way, she stopped to chat
with friends and neighbors
in that gray and damp old town
on the River Shannon.
What did they have to say?

Speaking in low voices
(the town was small —
news traveled fast),
one careless word
and there'd be hell to pay.

My grandmother wore
a round black hat
and, always, gloves.
She was very proper
in her way.

<48>

Irish Weather

"Andy, is it going to rain?"
my mother called from upstairs
and my father replied —
"Perhaps a few showers
later in the day —
bring your umbrella."

We all learned to read Irish weather,
clouds coming from the West
darkening the morning sky foretold rain.
Early sunshine, coming from the East,
drew from my father the comment
"It won't last."

By midday, clouds gathered,
raindrops tapped the window panes.
We were pessimists about good weather.
The Atlantic decided our many days of rain.
To protest this would have been in vain.

On our small island
on the edge of Europe
weather shaped our moods,
defined the lives we lived,
made us Irish, girls and boys —
emphasized life's sorrows and joys.

This poem has been alternately titled "Forecast."

<49>

Dear Daddy

Up on the hill, the wind
blows down the years
always blowing
where you used to be.

I have to think hard
to remember
the way you were
how you gently
placed seeds in our garden.

I asked their names —
"larkspur, antirrhinum,
snapdragons, verbena"
you replied,
your voice on
the ceaseless wind
in the cool Irish Spring.

You were very quiet —
as seeds inched
from your fingers
between little rills of earth.

Now when I go to the hill
the wind brings you near,
a gentle presence.
I stand at the gate
and see the old garden
you once tended
ablaze with flowers
and I hear your voice
on the wind,
naming their names.

<50>

Oracle (Early Version)

The last time I saw you
it was winter.
You picked your way
through shining pools of rain
on the driveway.
Forty years ago.

I do not think of you
lying in the quiet peace
of Dean's Grange. I see you
walking in the garden
at Gurrawn, looking
at the sky.

I asked you
"How do you foretell rain?"
and you told me,
"When a soft wind blows
from the West
and the mountains look close,
then we'll have rain."

And they came,
those quick Irish showers,
softly at first, spattering
on the rooftops —
a rush of sound, dashes of water
on the window panes
and a blackbird singing
in the ash trees.

No, I don't think
of Dean's Grange.
I think of the moment we shared
when you turned to me, smiling,
your gentle voice saying,
"Now, that's beauty,
isn't it?"

<51>

Oracle

For my Father
1896-1955

I remember you
walking in the garden
at Gurrawn
looking at the sky.

I asked you,
"How do you foretell rain?"
You told me,
"When a soft wind blows
from the West
and the mountains look close
we'll have rain."

And they came
those quick Irish showers,
pattering on the roof-tops,
a rush of sound
passing out to sea,
a blackbird singing
in the ash trees.

I think of the
moment we shared,
when you turned to me,
your gentle voice saying,"
"Now, that's beauty,
isn't it?"

<52>

My Father

Last time I saw you
It was raining.
I watched from the car
As you picked your way
Across the muddy lane.
It was winter
And I was leaving —
For another country.

You gave me one backward glance
From your Irish blue eyes —
Loving looks we exchanged.
I watched as you,
Stooping slightly
In your green coat,
Went through the gate
And away from me forever.

What tricks fate plays —
How was I to know
You carried within you
The seed of your destruction?
In less than three months
You would die
And I, far in another country,
Would silently weep over a telegram,
Handed to me by a stranger.

How would I know
I would not get the chance
To tell you how I loved you.
Because I am not sure
Of how I'll feel,
I've never visited your lonely grave.

<53>

Where Is My Father?

I put the question
to the waves, to the sky,
to the brooding woods.
I search for him
in places that he loved.
My progenitor.

I think of my father's
ancestors
and their fathers,
in and out of the dream.
They stand in the shadows
watching me.

From the green place
to the Rock at Dunamase
down the blood-line
to me waiting
by the sighing pines.
The sea, the sky, the woods —
these are all my father.

I must be silent and listen
for his voice on the easy wind.

<54>

Just a Moment

Only you could
tell me the names
each sound
like bells in the wind.

<55>

Welcoming the Wanderer

(Reapproaching Mark Strand's "The Man in the Tree")

ORIGINAL

I sat in the high tree limbs
A tree I had climbed when a child
A tree on a hill above the Irish sea.

Today a cold wind tossed the branches.
Between their limbs I saw you
slowly coming from the Killiney woods
your jacket open, wind tossed.

I watched you carefully, walking,
as you always did, even years ago
head up, eyes taking in the winter landscape
buffeted by the wind.

I did not move from my perch.
I wanted to see your smile
discovering me high above the meadows,
delighted, like a child, at your surprise.

Perhaps, now, you will tell me
why you went away — and where
you spent the intervening years.
I prepare to greet you.

<56>

VARIATION

Welcoming the Wanderer

I sit in the limbs of a tree,
a tree I had climbed as a child
high on a hill above the Irish Sea.

A cold wind tosses the branches.
I shiver as I watch you
coming through the Killiney woods,
your jacket open, wind tossed.

You walk carefully, head bent,
just as you did, years ago,
indifferent to the winter weather
and the roaring of the waves.

I do not move from my perch,
waiting to see you smile.
I'm seeing me high above the meadow
delighted to surprise you.

Can you tell me, now
why you went away
all these years — far from us,
indifferent to our tears?

<57>

Exiled

For my mother

Send me Irish earth.
I dream of it.
Steeped in the damp fragrance of roses,
the dying breath of summer
wafted from fallen crimson petals,
secrets of an Irish garden.

Send me leaves from Ireland,
I need them.
From the giant beech tree
rooted, sturdy by the grey stone wall,
tossed by an Irish wind
fresh from the storm-blown Irish Sea.

Send me a tear from Ireland
shed in a moment of remembering.
A little pearly token of love
from a tender Irish heart.

<58>

My Mother, My Ghost

In the quiet room on a shining summer day
windows open to the garden
a riot of flowers.

Afternoons you nodded off
in the old blue armchair by the fireplace.
Silence except for the birds
calling in the hedges.

One time staying there
on my yearly summer trip,
I went for a stroll
through the old neighborhood.

Coming back to the quiet house
I saw you sleeping,
hands folded in your lap.

When you heard my footsteps
you opened your eyes and smiled
as though I'd just returned
from a long journey.
I said nothing.

In my mind I see you
as in a faded photograph.
You wait, smiling
for loving words that did not come.

<59>

Farewell

For my mother, 1897-1987

You were sitting in your room
in the hazy Autumn sunlight,
your small figure in a pink robe,
hair tied with blue ribbon,
head bowed in sleep.

I closed the door behind me,
you opened your eyes.
Your smile held all your love,
accepting, unconditional, maternal.
Something I'll never see again.

I was not sure you knew
I had come to say good-bye.
You held my hand in yours,
soft and small
and said "I'll miss you."

We talked about the weather,
was it good for flying?
You had always had this fear —
the Atlantic weather
and the long flight from Ireland.

Evening cast dark shadows
on the walls of your room.
A nurse came to switch on lights.
I kissed you in the ordinary way,
as though this was a usual
"Good-night."

<60>

Soignée

You come into my room
sometimes — smiling.
Your blue linen
and the single string of pearls,
a skirt of fine tweed.
Someone once said,
Your mother is *soignée*."
I went home and looked up
that word in my French dictionary
and thought of you that way
ever since.

I remember once, when I was
over there
my yearly summer trip.
You were very old, alone
and lonely. One autumn afternoon
I went out for a stroll
through the old neighborhood.
When I came back to the house,
quietly coming into the room
with the crackling fire,
you were sleeping in the blue chair.
When you heard my footsteps
you wakened, opened your eyes
and smiled
as though I'd just arrived from a
long journey
in your dreams.

Now I know what I should
have said.

<61>

Voice

Is my voice like yours?
When I play the tapes
reading poetry
I am reminded of
you saying
"

<62>

Dickie

I did not know him.
Why does his name
evoke such emotion?
I see his picture in
my mother's old album —
bright-eyed in his
British uniform
hair neatly combed
(she told me he was 27
years old)[2]

---

[2] The poet's mother had been engaged to Dick McArdle, Royal Flying Corps, shot down over France in 1917.

<63>

Lost Love (Version 1)

My mother told me
of her love
all my life I knew
his name, Dickie —
and his English face shared
from sepia photographs
neat mustache, serious eyes
and that uniform
King Edward's Horse —
on one photo, later of my
mother
when she was nineteen
he wrote in perfect script
une petite diable
in another they stand
arm in arm, smiling —
a sunny autumn day
in the background
they were in the hay
all peaceful and serene
with hope
and then he left

my mother's love
died in 1917
fell from the skies
at Ypres Passchendaele
all these years between
I can't forget the little brooch
she gave me
when I was eighteen —
a keepsake, something to cherish

<64>

I lost it somewhere
in an old city
and now I can't forget
the man I never knew
whose gift I once possessed
and who, in the Great War,
fell from the skies
and perished.

<65>

Lost Love (Version 2)

I see your face
neatly mustached
hair smoothly slicked
over narrow forehead
the leather coat
like an armature.

You are not smiling.
There was little to smile about
in 1917.
On your left arm
the black ribbon
signifying loss.

As long as I recall
I've known you,
more than a name
my mother's lost love,
more than the old photograph
in my mother's album.

Behind you
the skeleton frame
the flimsy crate
that took you to your
early end.

<66>

Elegy for My Brother

For James, 1922-1988

I thought of you tonight
As I watched the bright moon
Rise in the Autumn sky.
I remembered last year
In the Wicklow hills
An October evening.
As the moon rose,
We scattered your ashes
By the rushing stream,
Carrigeenduff.

How you loved that place.
The silence of the hills,
The silver lake, your small house
Near the budding rowan trees.
Now you are part of that damp earth
Where the leaf mould in Spring
Nurtures violets,
Where you once turned to me and said,
"How can one see all this
And not believe in God?"
At Carrigeenduff.

<67>

Alignment

Tonight Venus and the moon
are in conjunction.
I thought of you, as I looked out
through the panes.
It's over a year now
since you died.
I thought of what you said
looking out over the lake
and the purple mountains
in the tremendous silence
of the Wicklow hills:
"How can one see all this
and not believe in God?"
And I was comforted and thought
all fits a pattern,
all is well.
As I looked through icy panes
at the cold moon and Venus
in brilliant conjunction,
I remembered the lake
shining among the trees
and the rushing stream
where we scattered your ashes
last October.
I thought of what you once said
in the tremendous silence.
You were beautifully aligned
with every season.

<68>

Loss

For my brothers

The surging seas rise and fall,
Casting a tremendous wall
Between us.

There is no recall —
That other place, that other time
Eludes me.

I breathe the pure air,
The dampness of mist on my cheek
Like tears.

Where the craggy coast receives the heaving sea,
The hilly paths forget we ever were,
And sorrow, loss of all the sweet familiar things,
Devours me.

And yesterday I heard
that you had died —
far away

I imagined in my childish fancy
I thought this insistent humming —
I'll never know what
prompted my imaginings —
what intimation of
the sadness
that life brings —
I only remember an Irish road
my small brothers
and the humming wires
like the voices of the many dead.

I thought "This is a sad sound"
sad but pleasurably so

<69>

Side by Side

Why do I remember
the dogs' barking
the sound carried to us
on the still evening air
as we stood above the valley
in Wicklow
long ago?

What is there of us
standing side by side
silent
listening to the sounds
of evening
on the hill
at Blessington?

<70>

Pianissimo

When my aunt lay dying
her poor, attenuated fingers
traveled across the linen
of the hospital bed.
She was a pianist.
Did she hear Chopin
in her head,
like an echo in an
empty room
upon which all light
has fled
and the years fell
away?
I watched beside her
her eyes closed
and suddenly she
opened her eyes,
turned her head.
"You are afraid of
the dark" she suddenly
said.
"It is nothing" — she
whispered
and drew a shallow breath
and then was dead.

<71>

Voice of Exile

Sometimes I hear the
lonely wail of a train
passing through the valley.
Especially at night
it evokes thoughts of
emigrants traveling west —
my Irish great uncle
nineteen years old
fresh from Ireland
twenty dollars in
his pocket, on the way
to Troy, New York.
Short, strong shoulders
a dark quiff of hair
over his forehead,
humorous dark eyes.

I imagine his trip up
the Hudson.
He'd never seen so big
a river —the one
near his home
in Roscommon
was small and quiet.
On this river ships ferried
passengers up to Albany.
He must have wondered
at the cliffs
rising along the water shore
and always the lonely
sound of the river
tearing at his heart,
carrying on the wind
the lonely sound of exile.

<72>

I Loved You Then

I loved you then
without knowing
that I loved you.
I loved your summer
days
when the evening sun
slanted through the trees
as through a stained-glass
window
lighting up your square
windows
with a rosy glow.
I loved the moment
when the
deep woods filled
with the soft *coo* of pigeons
and when, as evening fell,
flocks of crows swirled
above the trees to their
night roost in the old tower.

<73>

Patronymic

Sometimes,
with a shock of recognition
I see my old name
on a storefront, a truck,
a list of subscribers
to a favorite cause.
When I signed that old name
on correspondence, checks,
birthday cards,
I was another person,
counted myself one of many
with that name.
I remember the child
carefully writing out her name
first day at school —
the name was the person,
the person the name.
Just like that.
I considered it
a rite of passage
when I gave up my own, old name
for the name I was to use
for the rest of my life.

Rained Out Boulevard

I left you alone
in the warm house
electricity
in the air
from words unspoken

I went two miles
in the foggy evening
the rained out
boulevard
silent as a cave

Rivulets of water
trickled across
footpaths
spring leaves
embossed with crystals
grass shining
in the lamplight

I turned towards home
rehearsing apologies —
through the fog
I saw your familiar figure
waiting in the park

You came to me
and when we met
it was as if
the sun shone.

<75>

Sonas

For Jack

This autumn afternoon
a gentle breeze
stirs the leaves
of oak and maple.
From the window
I see the blue-gray
of a neighbor's roof
through chrome-yellow
foliage.

I'm reading Irish love poems
at the old table.
It is silent except
for the ticking clock
and your voice
downstairs
on the telephone,
quietly insistent.

Take hold of this moment,
take hold of it —
years from now
I will recall
the color of the leaves,
time ticking away
and the soft sound
of your voice
and know what *sonas*[3]
is.

---

[3] *Sonas.* Gaelic for "happiness."

<76>

Husband's Head

few hairs
shine of sunlight
pierces glass
bathes
gold
created
by nature.

Before Our Reuniting

I won't think about it
I don't want to get caught up
In that longing
That heart tearing

Love's Presence Has No End

Love's presence has no end
like air that flows unseen all about us
it fills the world with necessary force
that sustains life
helps us find joy in the scent of roses
in a stranger's smile
likes us all together despite strife,
and helps us onward daily, mile by mile.

<77>

Spirit

The guests depart.
I close and lock our door.
It is quiet now.
No sounds of voices
and laughter fills the air.

I look at your photo
on the far wall
where I placed it
years ago.

Why, at the happiest hours,
do I suddenly feel your presence?
It is as if your spirit
rejoices in my happiness.

At the Window

Was your ghost at the window
eyes the color of bluets?
Did you watch me
stoop and pick a last
blossom,
the flower they call innocence,
the color of your eyes?

<78>

Teddy

Old bear, you are
my link with childhood —
not mine, my son's.
You take me back
to a room in Ireland
thirty-three years ago,
blue-papered walls
the color of faded hydrangeas,
windows open
to a scarlet garden.
I hear my two-year-old
laugh when you fall
from his bed,
your protesting growl,
his voice, "Oh, Teddy,
Sorry."
Now your growl is stilled.
My son lives in Minnesota,
and you sit mutely
staring into space
in a corner
of my old rocking chair
in a corner of
my yellow
papered room.

<79>

Peter

When you were born
early in the A.M.
the swans flying over
Parnell Square
the roseate houses.

The day you were born
I saw three swans
flying over Parnell Square
the sun lit their wings
with a rosy light
reflected from the bricks
of eighteenth century houses.

You lay in your cradle
under a blue blanket
snug as a little
bee in a hive.

<80>

Johnny Doggy (A Mother's Tale)

In Washington Heights
on the way from the store
I lost Johnny Doggy
and saw him no more

He was the companion
of my little son, Pete
he wore a red coat
and black shoes on his feet

His eyes were like beads
his nose was a blot
he was only a doll
but we missed him a lot

The folks on the street
whom we questioned would say
"We ain't seen no doggy
coming this way"

Now to end a sad story
I questioned my son
(I know it's been ages
he's now thirty-one)
"Do you remember
a toy you once had
it was called Johnny Doggy
when you were a lad?"

He thought for a moment
and then shook his head.
"Johnny Doggy — don't remember,"
he casually said.

<81>

Masterpiece

For Peter

My son shows me a mushroom
big as a platter.
Skin gleams with the sheen
of finest olive oil.

About to be broiled
over glowing coals,
it is his tribute to summer,
an offering to friendship.

His tall figure leans
over the barbeque.
He wields a spatula
like a baton.
He is master of his art.

The mushroom cooks slowly,
juices make a small hiss
as they drip on the coals.
The air is scented with garlic.

Under the green umbrella
we watch as he lifts
this succulent gift
onto a wooden board,
slices it into even pieces.

Cordially he hands us
a small wedge,
his Portobello
his work of art.

<82>

Pete and Carla's Lad

For Jacob

I know a little fellow
Pete calls him "Binky Bee"
every time I meet him
he always smiles at me.

His daddy is a sweetheart,
his mommy is a gem,
when Binky Bee's all grown up
he'll be so proud of them.

Each time when I see Binky
he's grown an inch or two.
He calls us on the telephone
and greets us with *coo*.

Binky has such blue eyes
they sparkle like the sun.
Oh, folks, when you meet Binky
you're going to have such fun.

If each home had a Binky
the world would be so glad
for there's no one like dear Binky,
Pete and Carla's Lad.

<83>

For Joyce 1995

        I know I'm late —
        But please excuse.
        My reason is
        my hand's confused!

        You'll understand
        I really care,
        that's why I'm sending
        this sweet bear!

<84>

A Little Death

In memory of Pony, who died
Christmas Eve, 1993, aged 19.

There is no succoring
this cage of bones.
The coat, once glossy
is faded, matted, staring.
The claws no longer retract,
they provide traction now
for the failing legs.

She chooses her place to die
in the warm, dim corridor
where the light is kind.
I fill her bowl
with warm milk.
She cannot really drink,
just a faint lapping.

We gently stroke
the thin flank heaving
with each labored breath.
She responds, a small miaow —
I do not know how
I can face her end.

On Christmas Eve we leave
to celebrate an ancient story.
I offer up a prayer
"Oh, God, be kind to her,
make her going easy."
On our return she lies
as though in sleep,
eyes closed, thin legs
stretched out.
I stroke her fur
and weep.

<85>

In the Republic of Caring

A Poem for Friends

No one will pass
a soul
on the pavement
without pausing

at least
to speak a word of comfort,
also, after a while
no one
will lie on the pavement,

there will be
a place for everyone,
like birds
each will have a nest
of his own.

Children will respond
trustingly
to smiles from strangers,
on doors of houses
where harmony reigns

welcome signs
will mean what they say.
Less will mean more
and indulgence
will be unfashionable.

The air will be filled
with the resonance
of happiness,
the lion will lie down
with the lamb,

<86>

the anthem will be called
"Compassion"
the flag, a rose,
and no one will be alone
in the Republic of Caring.

<87>

Three Days Later

Three days I sat
bewildered by news
of a dear one's passing
gone like the warmth of summer
vanished like migrating birds

I try to settle my thoughts
as though they were objects
to be filed neatly away
in a closet drawer.
Like seeds buried in a garden.

<88>

A Small Remembrance

A ray of sunlight
strikes the glass dish
Last link with you
My childhood friend

I pass your empty house
Closed and silent
And I see you
Standing in the doorway
Giving me the gift

When the sun shines
This small keepsake
On my table by the window
Gives me back a glimmer
Like the sparkle in your eyes.

<89>

Rosebud

In memory of Diane Grund

A rose bloomed
late on the stalk
a little lamp
it lit the darkest
corner of the yard

unvisited by bees
uncaressed by butterflies
each morning
a leaf fell
from its fragile stem

windblown
it held its head
a fading
tender pink
against the evergreens

a killing frost
came like a knife
cutting the blue air
I raised the morning curtain
it was no longer
there

<90>

Neighbor

For Betty

Framed in the window
my neighbor sits reading —
tonight it is raining
a pool of light
reflected
in her wet driveway.

Each night she sits
at her kitchen table
glasses halfway down her nose
reading her German books
slowly turning pages —
she is very old.

There is something comforting
in this unvarying routine,
before I pull the shades
I take a long look —
then I hear the lonely whistle
of the train in the valley.

I deceive myself —
someday that light
will wink out and
I will look across the street
and wonder where she is.

<91>

Waterfall

I know a lady who lives alone,
she's always on the telephone
and calls me any time of day
and this is all she has to say.

Tommy H. has lost his mate —
Mrs. P. is filled with hate —
Johnny O. thinks only of money,
though sometimes he is very funny.

Mr. T. down at the Bank,
he is such a miserable crank.
Dr. H. has lost his touch,
these days no one sees him much.

At this point I've had enough,
I'm fed up with all this stuff.
I don't want to have a tiff.
She is a waterfall plunging over
the lip of a cliff.

<92>

Friends

Who comes at every
beck and call?
And would not let a
sparrow fall —
The Tiptons

Who answers every
cry for help
who hardly ever
thinks of "self"?
The Tiptons

Who greets each person
with a smile
and helps a stranger
mile by mile and does it all
with verve and style?
The Tiptons

Now as we honor them
today
we raise our glasses
and we say
"God Bless You"
and please always be
The Tiptons

<93>

Lost

We made the mistake again,
looking for Archie's house.
We took a right turn at Anderson —
perplexed, we wandered along Center
finally coming to Abbott —
there we met a mailman,
whistling as he walked.
We mentioned Archie's name
and his address.
The mailman wrinkled his forehead.
"Archie what, again?" he asked.
We spelled out Archie's name
The mailman smiled, a sad smile.
"Archie," he said, "A good guy.
He's gone from the block."

<94>

Estrella

Easy as you go,
Singer of songs.
To hear you
Reveals a core of strength
Each stanza said by you
Lingers in the mind
Like old ones sung
Around a flickering fire.

For John Trause

Jovial jokester, you strike
Odes that tickle the fancy
How much I'd like to hear
New verses from your sciomancy!

<95>

Voice Mail

I heard from an old friend
far away —
She didn't have a lot to say —
Only these few words
"I love you"
made my day.

<96>

The Flower and the Butterfly

Once the two of us were
like the flower and the butterfly
a gentle coming together
despite our differences —
now, alas, we are more like two bees —
an angry, albeit short, buzzing
when we are displeased.

<97>

Moving Up

For the children

Let us be a shining light
to those who come after us.
Let us strive to do what's right
and be the best we can be.

Let us remember this happy day
as we go forward on our way
to a future crowned by success
filled with joy and happiness.

Let us give the world a gift
our strength and pride and grit.
Let all who hear us now
know that this is our vow.

<98>

People

It Has to Do with Seeing

In memory of Charlie Brady

With an old friend
in a Dublin gallery,
I looked at a painting
sent from America —
a small cloud
in a blue sky
like a white sail
on a sapphire sea.

My obstinate friend
refused to believe
a single cloud
could float alone
in an expanse of
eternal blue.
Swore he had never
seen such a thing.

We argued, pro and con,
artistic imagination,
the perception of reality.
I told him what O'Keefe said:
"Nobody sees a flower, really.
It is so small and to see
takes time." I thought
'Nobody sees a little cloud.'

But this young painter
captured one forever,
caused my friend
to consider the possibility
that painting simply
has to do with seeing
and everything, however small,
has its own importance.

<101>

French Nails

The lady with French nails
languidly strokes
her honey-colored hair,
self-absorbed
she discusses her social life —
avec ennui.

Social nuances punctuate
her conversation.
She wearily informs me
of the latest
scandale de société
in New York.

With a *moue*, bored,
she mentions a certain name
not quite *de trop.*
The circles
in which she moves
are incestuously close.

With a fatigued air
she describes
yesterday's affair.
Confesses to a grand *faux pas* —
she was absolutely, positively
underdressed
for that *milieu.*

Meanwhile her hand
tipped iceberg white
endlessly caresses
les cheveux parfaits.
Her body, sinuous,
curved as if to strike.

<102>

When she takes her leave
the smile freezes on her lips —
her eyes are cold.
Her hand, an attenuated bone,
gives no hint of *amité*.

She says "Good-bye" —
I hesitate a moment, then
"Bonne chance, ma amie!"
I reply.

<103>

He Says!

"You are the apple
of my eye!"
I looked up *apple*
in *Webster's*,
it said:
"a tree having pink
and white flowers
and edible fruit."

I begin to feel myself
threatened
by this voracious love.
Will I be eaten up
and swallowed
chewed to a miserable core
tossed out?

I don't want
to be the apple
of anyone's eye.
I'd rather wither
on my own tree.

<104>

Sales Pitch

A sharp fellow,
quizzical eyebrows
blue suit, bow tie,
sells cars.
His determined patter
designed
to make me feel
deprived
or at least
inadequate.

Finger raised
condescending,
he reels off
statistics,
tells me gas
will be twenty miles
to the gallon.

New car smell,
the "thunk"
of a heavy door
is tempting —
but I refuse
to be seduced
by symbols.

I won't spend
forty-thousand
to be defined
by possessions.
He sees I have
no sense
of status
and dismisses me
with a high-beam
smile.

<105>

Lightweight, As in Superficial

He is a lightweight, she said.
Thus dismissed
he did not sink in my estimation.
Rather, as she is such
a heavy weight
I decided to encourage him.
He appeals much more
to my imagination.

<106>

Queen Bee

She was on the
fringe
of society
not so good
for her
id

through sheer
guts
and chutzpa
she
became a queen —
a new slant
on royalty

however
she fiddled
the loot
said
"only little
people pay taxes"

now the
party's over
and some
sad dame
has a new
slant
on fame

<107>

A.B.C.

The air smelled of eucalyptus.
A faint tinkle of water
dropped from a shell-like fountain
into a basin.
Three gold fish swam,
bodies flashing sunlight.

He rose up from a maze
of greenery,
Asian, tall, cheerful,
handsome, beaming
like some benign
nature god.

Over a pot of scarlet
hibiscus
I asked him
"Are you Chinese?"

Wrapping my flowers
with expert fingers,
twinkling, he replied,
"Yes, Ma'am, believe me,
I'm just good old A.B.C."

"A.B.C.?" From me.

"American Born Chinese."

<108>

Starting with a Line by W.S. Merwin

In the woods I came on an old friend hiking
and I asked him a question —
Do you find, in Nature,
an answer to life's problems?

He regarded me thoughtfully.
As he did so, a mourning dove
softly called in the trees
and soon, another answered.

My friend gently smiled.
"You see," he said, "there is no answer.
There is only acceptance
and in nature the consolation
of God's bounty."

I thanked him and went on my way.
Now I learn to receive each day
as a gift of grace and blessing.

<109>

Reds

The girl
with mussed hair
stepped into the diner
mini skirt
a blood-red flag
heels *tap-tap*
on the floor
a bag as big
as a sack
hung from her shoulder.

Seated
she ran a hand
crimson-nailed
through her coiffure
it looked electrified —
applied
ruby lipstick
to a generous mouth
settled back and
watched the door
expectantly.

A young man
entered
nonchalantly,
sporting
a scarlet Tee
that stated
defiantly
"Bolshevism."
He greeted her
off-handedly.

<110>

They ordered
French fries
and shared
a Coke.

<111>

Rap

Rap resonates
through rows
of gaudy clothes
gleaming green and gold
a screen of blue denim
washed out
like faded hydrangeas.
I wander
down the rows
as the rap beat goes
insistent, repetitive
move my feet to the beat
along the lines
of vivid robes.
I am old —
brilliant jackets
silver and gold
studded shirts
dazzling dresses
are not for me.
A thin boy
with a broom
sweeps the pristine room,
his long hair
sways as he moves
sweeping to the music.
Bored,
he stops to stare
at the busy
street.
He turns and
smiles
at me.
I know
what its like
to be
seventeen.

<112>

Oil Eater

What kind of guy
was driving along the highway
that summer afternoon?
Was he delivering something
somewhere or driving
just for the hell of it?

His rusty truck
two wooden doors, fit for a barn
tied with a rope rattled at the back,
an old tarp, laid on the roof
flapped in the breeze.

He wove through Mercurys
and Corvettes, to say nothing
of Jaguars and Mercedes.
He had an insolent air,
a kind of "don't give a damn"
attitude about the world.

Like a flag
a plume of blue exhaust
followed him along the highway.
His bumper sticker proclaimed —
"I may be slow
but I'm in front of you."

<113>

Confusion

Damn him
it's a crime
the way
he talks
always in the abstract
I feel like a wisp
it's enough to make me
hate conversation

How can I
diffuse his flights of fancy
I'll down snifters of brandy
brandy's pretty concrete stuff
maybe it'll move him
to mirth
hey how about a little mirth
with your brandy

I think I've had
one drink too many
I'm going back to
solitude
that's what comes of
deep conversation

<114>

Early Morning Encounter
With the Entomologist

Hi!
Let me tell you something —
ants dance on larkspur
stay brave in rain
set Canterbury bells
trembling
walk upside-down on stems
gnaw wood in houses
create havoc in choirs
many possess a pedicle
not to speak of a thorax
I could mention *Zoraptera*
all from the family
Formicidae
and of course
they all communicate silently.

Ok! Ok!
Personally
I'd appreciate
more simplicity
in language —
So shut up!

<115>

Harriet's Diet

Harriet, no longer pleasantly plump,
Decided she looked an awful frump,
Embarked on a diet, monotonous,
But Harriet decided she'd slim or bust.

Harriet's husband observed with dismay,
The shelves fill up with what looked like hay,
The menu changed from rich to poor
And Harriet's moods became mighty sore.

Weeks went by and Harriet suffered,
Her husband came home to an empty cupboard,
Sharp words were exchanged almost every day,
And Harriet's looks went all astray.

After six weeks Harriet looked,
Not quite like what they say in books,
Her bones stuck out through her snow-white skin,
But you've got to suffer to be thin.

Harriet's husband slept alone
Rather than be stabbed by Harriet's bones.
What a pickle they both were in,
All because Harriet yearned to be thin.

When Harriet wafted through the house
Weighing scarcely more than a good-sized mouse,
Harriet's husband, whose name was Jim,
Decided action was up to him.

Sat down and said, "My sweet, dear wife,
Being slim is good but what is life
When concentration is all on one issue?
There's more to it than being thin as a tissue."

<116>

And he decided there and then,
To go out and buy a Purdue hen,
Cooked the dinner and set the table,
Just to show Harriet he was able.

Now Harriet's ways were a bit duplicitous,
She wasn't really such a masochist,
But she had her own ways of obtaining her wishes,
And now Jim even washes the dishes.

The lesson from this is plain to see,
Everyone needs variety,
Drastic means are sometimes needed,
To have our unspoken wishes heeded.

<117>

Arrangement in Gray and Black

Early one morning
the depressed gent
donned his tweed coat
slid into his shoes
close with twine
(he was frugal and saved string)
tossed a scarf
about the nape of his neck
gave a nod to the dog,
put a rag in his pocket
(in case of accidents)
and some extra tissues
and set off
through the mud
for the Lovers' Leap.
When he reached the cairn
he met his twin
who said, in answer to his question,
"No dice."
So our gent walked home
turned on the gas
put his head in the oven
and took a permanent nap.

<118>

Marked Man

I can never bare my arms —
due to the foolishness of youth
emblazoned above my elbow
there's an Irish leprechaun
feisty as Irish rain.

I remember my parents' comments
chilling, sarcastic, disapproving
and their solemn warning
"Someday, my dear, you'll regret ..."
and I laughed it off.

Now I'm restrained
by this long pride
to long-sleeved shirts
and long-sleeved sweaters.
Winter and summer
I have a secret to hide.

<119>

To a Man Tying His Shoes

A daily ritual —
shoe lace tying time.
He sits on the lowest
step of the stairs
socks pulled up
neatly together
bent over
left foot forward
right foot in a dancing position
laces tugged to ensure
both even and taut
then bowed and tied
in a neat knot.
A sigh.
He gives a satisfied glance
considering a task well done
and gravely faces the
audience of one
awaiting her applause.

<120>

Two Old Men Walking

Look at them
two old men
walking
every day
in the little park
like twins
small, shrunken
in tweed coats
carrying canes
eyes big
through the powerful lens
of their glasses
a certain innocence
about them
old pals

they walk
a few steps
by the kiddie swings
then stand
heads nodding
in comment
and assent

<121>

Bargain Basement

The worn faces of poor women
Fingering dresses in the bargain basement
Sadly checking the price tags
Of warm winter clothes.

<122>

Over the Tool Rack

I'm studying the
tools on the stone shelves
when I hear the
baritone, the Russian syllables
a man and woman
an old fur coat
unfashionable style
and pants too long
and flared
they converse in low
voices —
and I see the price
is too high —
think of what they
came from — all
that weight of
appalling history
old enough to have
been children in the
war and I can't
know their experiences
their lives
kindness to strangers
we all walk like the
man who carried
his shadow
pursued by shadows
lucky to have gotten
this far,
our lives touched
by a smile
over the tool rack.

<123>

White

My friend loved her white shoes
Only to be worn in summer,
They had heels inches high
And pointed toes like the heads of needles.
The problem was —
she could only manage a few steps
at a time — then sat down suddenly
and heaved a sigh.

One day we suggested a walk
In my friend's garden.
She demurred, politely
the excuse, fatigue after a long day.
We strolled among the flowers
conversation flowed, laughter rose
our friend sat at the windows — watching.

<124>

Pocket Book

My friend's white pocket book
Stands on the table — plump and stuffed
I think of it when it was new —
Containing only a comb and small purse
All signifying a new beginning —

Then, over time the pocket book
swelled with myriad items —
some put purposefully, some for memories
to savor in the future,
some to get rid of, somewhere, sometime.

I think of life like this
starting with small special items
some not useful or needed in the daily chores
then gradually one accumulates things
we think we cannot do without.

<125>

Discretion

Over the parking lot
of the food market
a new moon, lemon slice,
trailed by a brilliant star.

I wanted to stop
a busy passer-by
point heavenwards
share my sense of awe.

Then I thought
why spoil this moment
of enchantment
to invite comment
that may only jar.

<126>

Nice Day!

Some folks have faces
like iron signs on grassy lawns
that warn "KEEP OFF."
Their eyes avoid contact,
mouths set in grim lines.
They never smile.
What disaster has befallen them?
Did the cat not return last night?
Is the pain of corns ruining their day?
Did that check not come in the mail?
A simple "Hi" is not returned,
they have no desire for camaraderie.

I want to say —
"Lighten up, folks, it's Spring."
Twigs of forsythia joyfully bloom,
little gusts of wind bring
the scent of damp earth,
birds sing choruses of praise,
nights, stars blaze in the sky.
Folks with disgruntled faces
pass through this world
like clouds that cross the sun
causing us to look up and say —
"Only a cloud, folks,
it's still a nice day."

<127>

Games

In the old school yard
The nuns devised a game —
Each child given
A paper with a name,
Each paper different,
No two the same.
Pin on each back —
Each girl to guess the name
The nuns gave her —
In navy dress, black stockings
Shy and awkward she stood
Perplexed; the game ended.
What am I? What's my name?
A friend removed the paper —
All exclaimed "Mollusk."
What is that? Strange, that name —
Hours later, in the dictionary
She found the simple explanation —
"MOLLUSK" — a spineless creature.
Then she wept.

<128>

Plastic

Once, when a child,
my father referred
to a fashionable neighbor,
always dressed to kill, as
"that plastic woman."

In the Ireland
of my childhood
there was little plastic
to be seen.
China was the word
I used to hear.

One day at school
I asked my teacher
"What is plastic?"
She answered
"Fake china."

I am still confused.

<129>

Rye

Walking by the shore at Rye
I watch the wheeling gulls
observe the still ponds
inland
their reed grasses stirred
by the breeze.

This autumn day
all is tranquil here
almost as tranquil as
when the English jailors
first came to explore
the Piscataway.

Here between two universities
I wonder why they made
the voyage —
endured the weeks at sea.

I try to imagine them
the lookout shouting
the sun dazzling to the west.

Eastwards the heaving seas
westwards stretches
the unbelievable space
to America
where everything was
possible.

<130>

JFK

and then that funeral
the black hearse symbol
of a fallen hero
and the small figures of
the children in their very proper
attire
on the steps

it was autumn
that sad month
when the sky foretold
shorter days
summer had gone
somber voices
the sound of drum beats
and the "Irish" president
was laid to rest.

<131>

Light Touch

Sure, you had to go
but the dusting could've waited.
How was I to know
the damn bowl
your mother left you
would break
when I touched it?
I know you said
be careful and I was —
last time I broke something
you hit me on the head!
I'm a welder, for Chris'sakes
dusting ain't my thing!

He'd better not think
because he cussed me out
I'll dance a jig before him.
I'll make him feel like a worm.
I'll make him squirm.
The crude dude!
He'd better change his mood.

He says working in construction
bites his bones.
I told him
take vitamins
but no, he says
he ain't no sissy.
Then I say, don't groan —
but I'm mad about that bowl.
He says he ain't done nothing
says he wakes every morning
to the sound of birdbrain!

I'll show him who's boss —
he'll say he's sorry!

<132>

Love

Love is so vulnerable
Love cannot stop the rot
Love alone is powerless
Slaves loved their children
Over in Germany children
of loving mothers vanished
in the fire.
Love needs reinforcing.
Love needs the lilt of steel
to reinforce itself.

<133>

Titanic at Belfast

"To build or not to build"
that was never the question.
Over one hundred years ago
on a windy March day
three thousand men worked
showed the way to build a hull,
laid the keel of the ship
to be named *Titanic*.

Launched May 31, 1911 —
the largest moving manmade
object in the world,
the epitome of the shipbuilders' art
built by the men of northern Ireland.
Her name, all too soon,
would become part of history.

An onlooker spoke of her
"as more like an imperial yacht
than a passenger liner."
In the shipyard at Belfast
hundreds of men
cheered as her keel was laid,
cheered again her maiden voyage.

<134>

Far across the North Atlantic
with a sound like thunder
a mountain of ice broke off
from its parent glacier
and began its slow drift
towards the sea lanes
of the North Atlantic.

I asked Moira to write a poem about Titanic *for consideration
in the 2012* Sensations Magazine *issue. Notes and line
numbering, in Moira's handwriting and using her typical
writing/editing process, were found in a folder on her writing
desk in September 2010. I'm certain these notes did not exist
before 2010, so this is likely her most recent poem — and her
use of the word "over" in line 3 implies that this poem was
written after March 2009. —DM*

<135>

The Literary Life

Just Like Jane

I take a book
from my bookcase
out scrambles
the thinnest spider,
pale yellow.
Slips across *Sanditon*
hesitates at *Persuasion*
races to *Emma*
disappears behind
Sense and Sensibility.

Between pages sixteen
and seventeen
of *Mansfield Park*
lies a crushed moth,
leaf-thin,
silver wings
gracefully folded
in a humble
prayerful position.

I have no doubt
that the deceased
was part of
the spider's
winter larder.
Was it
just like Jane —
deliciously simple
or simply delicious?

<139>

For Emily Brontë

A dry cough
sounds on the stairs
halting footsteps
along the flagged passage.
The candle's flicker
casts a thin shadow
on the white walls.
The dogs' dinner
readied —
the task must be done
before the clock
strikes six.
The wind skirls
off the moors.
Windows rattle.
In a quiet corner
the spider
weaves its net
undisturbed
by the dying candlelight.
Down the narrow passage
a door
is gently closed.

<140>

No Place for Emily

It is autumn in Amherst.
Alone on a bench in Emily's garden
I look at the red brick house,
think of the white dress
hanging in simple folds
in her old bedroom upstairs.

I hear a door open and close.
What to do if she comes
down the narrow path by the hemlocks?
Perhaps she'll greet me with a smile
or a line of lyric verse,
or will she dismiss me, an intruder?

In the shrubbery's tinted leaves
sparrows gently flutter.
Behind the trees that line Main Street
the rushing sound of cars.
In the distance a bell chimes.

A plane thunders overhead.
The small ghost flees
to the sheltering walls,
her safe old home.
This age has no place for Emily.
She belongs in quiet memory.

This poem has the alternate title of "In Emily's Garden."

<141>

Homestead

It is Autumn in Amherst.
Sitting alone on a bench
in Emily's garden
I see the summer flowers
fading fast.
In the shrubbery birds flutter.
Otherwise, silence.

I look at the red brick house
and think of her bedroom,
the narrow bed, the small desk.
Her white dress, like a bride's,
hangs in simple folds.
Tokens of remembrance.

I half expect her to come
down the narrow path
under the hemlocks.
Perhaps she'll greet me
with a smile and a line
of enigmatic verse,
or, seeing me a stranger,
she will flee to her life
of seclusion.

This is a revised version of the poem alternately titled "No Place for Emily" and "In Emily's Garden."

<142>

Thoreauesque

I never go to the movies
hardly watch TV —
It's all too much for me
Life lived at a remove
from a reality I crave
I want to live in a simple place
near woods
where I can walk and
listen to what's in my head
and hear birds and the rustle of leaves
and transcend the whole world
be where birds sing
and there is, otherwise, silence.

<143>

The Goats at Connemara

The goats come slowly —
daintily walking
to the wire fence,
daintily picking their steps
through the rough grass of the pasture.
They butt their heads gently

inviting a scratch on a finger
petting their skulls.
They are the offspring of Paula's
herd carted here from
Michigan
the spring of 1945.
This is their home — a place
of pilgrimage
when the aging poet
wrote and dreamed
looking across the valley
towards the blue slopes of
the Smokies.[1]

Did he, in his work room under
the eaves,
hear them bleating
as I do now,
scratching their rough pates
and thinking of a
voice stilled, a family gone
a house empty
only these few friendly
animals a reminder
of the man.

---

[1] This poem refers to Connemara, the North Carolina farm owned by poet Carl
Sandburg from 1945 until his death in 1969.

<144>

Courtesy

Seton Hall, West Orange, NJ, 1992

That evening the poets
lauded Whitman
in learned, witty phrases.
The old poet,
dead one hundred years,
would have been amused.
After the ceremony
the guests gathered,
wine glasses clinked.
I knew no one there.

I stood by a window
watching rain falling
on a secluded lawn.
A thin man with kind eyes
joined me. He asked —
Do you know what Whitman called grass?
I shook my head.
Smiling, he said,
The handkerchief of the Lord,
a nice phrase.

We looked out
at the vernal lawn,
speaking of Whitman
and the shining grass.
What is your name? I asked.
He smiled and bowed
Merrill, he said
then left to join the party crowd.

One variation of this poem was published under the title
"Remembering Merrill." See the "Variations on a Theme"
section of this volume for a 2010 version.

<145>

Mending Glass

*On reading Derek Walcott's Nobel Prize
Acceptance Speech, 1992*

I broke an heirloom.
When it was whole
I took its symmetry for granted.
Piecing together
the shattered fragments,
now my love is stronger.

This vase, repaired,
is all the more precious.
I see in each shard
though flawed, a sealing
of its original shape —
a new kind of perfection.

Poetry is like that,
assembling and reassembling
pieces fashioned
from fragmented memory.
Making and remaking
line by plaited line.

<146>

Brodsky Reads

Dublin, June 1992

His voice resonates
through the Georgian church.
He recites from memory,
explains that translation
"lags behind
the original work."
At times he fluffs a word;
in his accented English
repeats a haunting stanza,
exhibits a kind of
controlled fury.
My fellow Dubliners,
books in hand, follow
line by line.

He traces his odyssey —
Leningrad, Norenskaya,[2]
then destiny — America.
Outside, swallows swoop
over rooftops,
their distant twitter
a lively counterpoint
to his heroic oratory.

The reading ends.
With a shy smile
he accepts applause.
In a generous scrawl
he signs my book,
misspells my name,
and then, this hero,
this survivor,
walks off with
my favorite pen.

---

[2] *Norenskaya.* A Soviet labor camp.

<147>

Current Events

Laura Bush decided "NO"
Peaceful poetry would not go
And with one resounding blow
Canceled White House poets show
Now our words against war flow

<148>

Reading

Basking in the adulation
Of poetry junkies
The poet smiles ecstatically
Adjusts his papers
The reading commences.

The more revelatory the poem
The greater the applause.
An element of prurience here
The shock effect
Confessional will have
Temperatures raised
By cheap thrills.

The evening drones by.
I'm blocking out
the four-letter words
the detailed physical agenda.

Beaming with smiles
of self-satisfaction
the poet goes on
to the next event.
The modest demeanor
is deceptive.
Ego here is the *raison d'être*.
I'll reserve my comment
until later.

<149>

St. Valentine's Day Massacre

Why are these people so alone?
For what great crimes do they atone?
Or are their noses out of joint
Because they, sadly, do not vaunt
Sympathetic personalities?

Reading her rhymes,
I ponder why one's
Loneliness "beats at the back"
Of her eyes.
Is is because she cannot be
The kind who appeals to you and me?

Why is one half-wit "invisible"?
Surely these lines are faintly risible.
Another moans in Atlantic City,
Distinctly an occasion
To be witty.
But no, it's nothing but
Crass self-pity.

What problem has the single male
Who really is beyond the pale —
"Hugging a beast"
What uncouth endeavor —
I'd banish him to hell forever.

Oh, help us Lord, we're lost at best
To fathom poets Q, R, and S.
They obviously write with passion
But soon they'll be right out of fashion,
As is the case with everyone
Who writes to order
Not for fun.

<150>

Aversion to *I*

I have an aversion to *I* —
so often, in conversation
it denotes self-absorption
when overused
in friendly intercourse —

I should be used sparingly
in appreciation, in love, in understanding
I should caress, should appreciate
should praise the good,
condemn the bad.

Yes, use *I* sparingly
Thus used, it is a tool for friendship
not an intrusive ego word —
like a steel beam in architecture
it holds friends together.

<151>

Writing Class

I hurry from the house
to the small room
where young people sit
expecting me to give
some meaning to their lives
their eyes sadly fixed
on me

I listen to them trying
to express the inexpressible
perhaps all they need
is someone who will listen
as their thoughts
slowly spill out
into the shadowy room

<152>

Poetry Class

Windows glisten
with silver raindrops.
Main Street gleams;
in gutters water streams.

In the spacious room
we sit and talk
of many things.
Our words have wings.
Today they fly away.

Let's try to catch them
as they fall from heights unknown
and fashion them in poems
that we will write at home.

<153>

Consanguinity

Once upon a time
a short-sighted girl
with flaming red hair
and a dictatorial mother
was made to wear a red cap —
she hated her mother
and she hated the cap.
She decided to go
for a walk in the woods
where her grandmother lived.
She didn't love her grandmother
but she decided
to visit her.

When she arrived
the door was off the latch —
Grandma was in bed
muffled up to the chin.
"Why are you in bed?"
asked the girl.
Grandma answered in a low voice,
"Why do you think, dummy?"
This kind of retort
was one of the reasons
the girl hated her grandmother.
"I can hear," she said,
"you have a bad cold."
"Nuts to you," snapped Grandma.

The girl decided
that kindness wasn't working.
She went to the kitchen
and got a large knife —
she hid it behind her back
and went into the bedroom.

<154>

Grandma made a growling sound.
"I have a cure for your cold,"
said the girl.
She plunged the knife
into Grandma's hairy breast.

The moral of this tale —
never take children
for granted.

<155>

Rutherford

I stand outside your home
and try to imagine you, doctor/poet
writing your poems, a new style
between tending to your patients.
What kind of man were you?
Dedicated to two professions —
doctor to the poor, singer of lyrics
both a reaching out to folks.

Gone forty years, your voice silenced.
But, in the schools of America, I trust
teachers bring your magic
to those who will learn your lines,
a new generation
who will smile at "The Red Wheelbarrow."

<156>

Memento

Coming from a reading
in the old library
my head is full of poetry.
On the way to 95
I see the sign *Ridge Road*
and think of Williams.

Over the Meadowlands
a plane
flying into Teterboro,
flash of silver
framed by blue sky.

He would have made a poem
from this.
The significance of blue and silver,
poetry, the language of being,
and our voices echoing
in the empty room,
back in Passaic.

*A variation of this poem was published with the title
"Allegory."*

<157>

Starting with a Line from Emily Dickinson

A door just opened on a street.[3]
I turned my head to see
And watched a scene of joyousness
That had not to do with me.

Now when I travel by that path
I look upwards at the sky.
It's there that I find happiness.
My spirit questions — why.

---

[3] Opening line is from "Part One: Life CXI" from *The Complete Poems of Emily Dickinson* (1924).

<158>

On Reading Wendell Berry's *Sabbaths*

I lay my hand on your book
and feel strength flow from it,
the strength of what you describe
in its pages —
of woods and fields,
of water and flowers,
of wild things.

As I read your poems
I feel something in my heart
that brings me near to tears,
because despite the strength
of Nature's blessings
and the treasures that it holds,
in our arrogance and ignorance
we have squandered this inheritance
and pillaged Nature
down the years.

<159>

Monsoon of Inspiration

I wait for a monsoon
of inspiration
when the slow filling
of the wells of thought
will brim over
and, like a fresh draught
of water
after a thirst
I will find inspiration
at the walls of ——

<160>

Nature

Bird and the Sea

On a painting by Morris Graves
at the Montclair Art Museum, NJ

The gaze poignant.
Big, wistful eyes brood
in an unwinking stare.
The beak fierce
but this bird is vulnerable,
it has no protection
against the elemental rage
of the sinister sea.

It crouches, waiting,
talons grasping a rock
by the moonlit winter waters.
The paint strokes
hint at a turbulence hidden,
menacing.

What was Graves saying?
Is his bird a symbol
of us all, part of a mystery
of fragile, transient life
standing at the edge of darkness
as clouds obscure the moon?

<163>

Brush Stroke

Birds are printed
against the sky
splints of flowers
splinters of light.

<164>

Allta[1]

Walking these hills
I thought of your story.
Out of the autumn sky
a goshawk flew before you
as you wandered above Lough Dan.

You heard a chaff whistle.
Nearby, on the gray lake,
a lone duck swam.
Save for a little wind
all else was silent.

Then, you told me,
the goshawk landed
on a moss-covered stone,
fixed you with its
stern, yellow eye.
Mysterious.

Observing this northern bird
you stood absolutely still.
Suddenly it swooped
above your head, its call
a strange, harsh cry,
as if to tell you —
"You are disturbing
my earth, my world,
my sky."

A variation of this poem was published with the title "Feral."

---

[1] *Allta.* Gaelic for "feral."

<165>

Iolar

"Young American Bald Eagle
strays across Atlantic."
— *Irish Times*, November 1987

Hurled by the wind
into the womb
of the dark wood
the storm-swept
navigator
touched land
among the roaring
trees.

Great wings drooping
the massive bill opened
on a raging thirst
the great claws — fish catchers —
grasped the wet earth.

A slow surge of light
broke over Ireland
emptied the sky of stars.
The weakened bird
sank in upon itself
prepared to die.

The natives walking
their familiar woodlands
came upon this stranger
succored her and
in the language
of that place
named her
"Iolar."

*The above poem also has been
published under the title "Landfall."*

<166>

Quabbin

"Adventurous eagle soars free at Quabbin."
— *Boston Globe*, February 1988

Distant lakes reflect
the dazzling sky
winter sun
strikes stars in the snow
the woods
a dark sanctuary.

The symbol of freedom
carried
to the highest hill
the American wanderer
sent home
from the distant island.
The assembled citizens
watched silently.

Uncaged —
a hesitant step
the stern eye
scans the wintry landscape
curved beak a scimitar
feathered talons imprint
the snow.

A pause
at the precipice —
then wings flattened
an upward soaring
on streams of air
pursued by her shadow
on the polished ice
Iolar flies
gone beyond echo
into the enclosing sky.

<167>

Ceircín

Light washes the landscape.
A breeze like a sigh
from the distant sea
stirs the clusters of elder,
night drains from the sky.
The yard below my window
is silent.

A pea-hen shyly steps
from the dusk of the hayshed
into this morning world.
Her fan-shaped crest
neatly furled, demeanor modest.
A small black cat follows,
tail erect like a banner.

With a harsh *caw*, a crow leaves
the sheltering trees,
flies westwards.
Some secret law determines
where it goes.
Cat and hen do not raise their eyes,
they have their own concerns.

A woman in a blue apron
comes down the garden path
holding a pan of food.
She calls, softly, in Irish —
Ceircín, Ceircín.
The pea-hen raises her crest
in salutation.

Cat and bird touch
beak to nose, a gesture
tender as a lover's kiss.
I watch this amiable pair
bend their heads and feed
from the yellow dish.

<168>

Jersey Spring

I watch turkey vultures
soar in the spring sky.
I do not ask why
I am uplifted.
Their endless circling
is a spring ritual
in the Jersey countryside.

They soar over woods
where trees budding now
are soon to be filled
with returning avian migrants.

<169>

Canadas at Overpeck

Through the leafless trees
I see them
assembled on the lake
mirrored on the still water —
Canada geese.

Companionably they float
wing beats
like the beat of a heart
slow like their flight south
following the sun.

They come to the lake
every autumn
this convocation of birds
a sort of benediction
on the days of waning light.

They follow the wheel
of the seasons
this instinctual search
for the places of the sun
and the winter growth.

As I watch from the shore,
they rise, honking,
in a flurry of wings
they circle the water
spiraling into the sky.

Minutes later all I can see
is a thin skein
like a wisp of smoke
fading in the evening air —
the lake is as if they were never there.

<170>

Passage at Overpeck

The Canadas have
passed this way again.

Through the leafless trees
I see them
gathered on the lake
mirrored on the still water.

Sociably they cluster
wing beats
like the beat of a heart
slow like their flight south.

They come to this lake
every autumn
a benediction
on the days of waning light.

They follow the wheel
of the seasons
searching for a warmer sun
and a winter growth.

I watch from
the shore and
they rise, calling
spiraling into the sky.

All I can see
is a thin skein
like a wisp of smoke
fading in the evening air.

<171>

Geese Pass

The geese pass
this way again.

Through leafless trees
I see them
gather on the still lake.

Wings pounding
like the beat of a heart
slow like their flight south.

They come each autumn
a benediction
on the days of waning light.

They follow the wheel
of the seasons rising
spiraling, searching
for a warmer sun.

All I see
is a wisp of smoke
fading into the evening sky.

<172>

A Question

I stand by the creek
at Overpeck —
Across the blue Spring water
I see a swan, watching.
As I come down
to the water's edge this bird
comes hurrying towards me
wings opening and closing
black feet paddling —
I remember I had read
a few days before,
how someone, somewhere
had killed a swan —
is this its mate
looking up at me?
Did it hope that I would solve
the mystery
of her loneliness?
I ask myself
what do swans do
when their mates
are no longer there?
Then this swan
slowly paddled across the lake
to where the Canada geese
might provide
a little company.

<173>

The Two Swans

Pavlova & Jack, 1926

The great dancer
Anna Pavlova
had a pet swan
named Jack.
She was sufficient
company.
Jack often came
and placed his
neck in her lap—
Fruitless thought—
It could mean nothing
to this swan
whose living habitat and being
even the lonely lake couldn't heal—
his companion gone
he seeks answers
wherever he can find them

Jack, 1931

I wondered if, like
Anna Pavlova,
I had my very own swan
as she had.

I remembered a picture
of the dancer posing,
arms around the
sleek curved neck of Jack
her very own swan.

When Anna died
did Jack mourn?

Swans mate for life,
I once read.

<174>

Medieval

I run to the castle
under a scintillating sky
pursued by the unicorn
which swiftly gallops
over the rain-soaked
ground

I quickly lock the door
hold a mirror
to observe the beast
galloping in circles
in the meadow
its panting
is horrific

A man comes
to the edge of the woods
carrying a silver bow
shoots the animal
its blood drips
like red poppies
in the emerald grass

Rain spits
on the window
obscures the view
I slowly draw the curtains
try not to listen
a high-pitched scream
spirals toward
the sky

<175>

Quick Swing of a Broom

"The poor beetle, which we tread upon
in corporal sufferance feels
a pang as great as when a giant dies."
—*Measure for Measure*, XXX.1.85

The man in his garden
stuns the industrious bee,
the proud gardener spreads
poison against insects
and the birds suffer,
while my neighbor
with one whack of a broom
killed a mouse.

She brought
forefinger and thumb together,
said "It was very small,"
told how the mouse
hid under a chair,
described how she took
the broom and how the creature
raced from corner to corner
of her room.

Was this a mother mouse
foraging for her brood,
seeking a pittance from
my neighbor's pristine house
as doom descended
in the quick swing of
a broom?

I thought of my neighbor's
farming ancestors
in the German Middle Ages,
piling sacks of grain
after the hard work
of the harvest.

<176>

What atavistic impulse
caused the triumphant gleam
in my neighbor's eyes?
She had no granary to protect.

She said she lifted the mouse
on a shovel,
put it out into her garden.
"There was a drop of blood
on its head," she said.
"A drop of blood
ruby red."

An earlier version of this poem was titled "Mouse."

<177>

Little Black Ant

Today, coming in
from the garden
I stepped on a small creature
hurrying across my floor.

I lifted it
on a piece of paper.
One leg was missing,
little clubbed antennae
waved in frenzy,
small jaws gaped.
Was it sending out frantic pleas —
"Where is my world?"

I once read the Chinese
characters for "ant"
symbolize unselfishness,
justice, duty —
a sociable creature.

I thought of the plight
of this sociable creature,
shuddering,
head bowed to thorax,
legs curled against its abdomen.
All defenses gone,
its small agony nothing
to the world.

On what errand was it bound?
I know the little black ant's
predilection for sugar.
Was its destination
my open sugar bowl?

<178>

One last shudder and life fled.
In the tender green of early spring
I laid this minute corpse.
Vigilant sextons wait,
in the crevices of the earth.
They'll carry their brother
to some humble, secret crypt.

<179>

Ode to a Boy with a Hare

      In the light of autumn
      on the highway,
      a child
      holding up in his hands
      neither a flower
      nor a lantern
      but a dead hare.

<180>

The Sadness of Animals

Dogs, met on the pathway
Look into your face
With a seeking look
Is this a friend
Or a foe.

Personification

I'm his pretty dog —
when he sits by the fireplace
on winter evenings
I climb onto his lap,
settle down and snore.

It's another story with her —
as soon as breakfast is over
she calls my name from the kitchen
and announces "Time for walkies."
I sigh and obediently come.

Outside, in winter, she marches
along the chilly sidewalk.
I trot freezing paws,
held by the leash in her hands.

<181>

Burial of the Wood Thrush

I saw your pale
breast among tan leaves
songbird.
What stilled your song
one spring
one summer?

From the egg —
obeying the summons
to fly south —
I saw you
a few days
rustling up leaves
under the hedge
when the prowler came.

Did your heart beat
more than ever
a minute?
Did your voice shriek
out in terror —
or was there only a
silent struggle
as the prowler took your life?

I stroke the dainty features
examine the fine-honed wings.
I'm robbed of
the flute-like phrasing
of your song
fine singer.

<182>

The children point a finger,
gently stroke the soft breast.
Upper wing covers
smooth to your sides.
The neck is broken.
The head falls to one side
droops as though sorrowful.
So short a life.

The tough pigeons stroll
along my path.
Only a squirrel pauses
in astonishment.
I watch as it turns
you over with its paw,
touches you.

Were you too preoccupied
rustling the leaves
to notice the marauder?

<183>

Seal

I remember
when we rowed out onto the sound
singing "The Bold Remain Men"
then a slight darkening of the water
at the side of the boat.
The sleek head of a seal surfaced
big eyes in a whiskered face
gazing innocently at us two.

Slowly it swam in circles
as we backstroked the oars
and I sang softly
my song over and over again.

We did not talk.
Only the gentle splash
of the oars
the clear blue water of the sound
the grassy island
with its little church and
bulky tower.

Nothing else —
just those eyes
a little glacious
looking at us
our gaze
our oars barely stirring the shining water.

<184>

We pull in to the island's cove
where the strip of sand holds us
we look back
it is still here
its gaze a question
who are you — why are you here —
or perhaps
there is something between us
but neither you nor I
can ever know
how to know.

<185>

The Seeker

For my brother, Jim

He went to the mountains to seek God,
and found Him in the beauty of a blade of grass.
God's glory shone in the morning sun,
and in the tranquil evenings
He breathed peace on the hills.
Not a day did pass,
but a part of Nature's aspect
showed His face.
In each leaf he found a trace
of that great Spirit,
so remote,
and yet so near to those who seek.
In the birds' swift passings
across a mackerel evening sky,
he saw His glory.
In the rushing stream,
His voice rang out, a glad shout
of joy in His creation.
In the piercing sweetness of early spring,
he found Him in the gentle snowdrop
braving the cold by the giant beech tree.
And the fallen feather from a blackbird's wing
reminded him that all His creatures
are of concern to Him.

<186>

Music

The stream runs clear to its stones.
I sit alone by its flow.
The sunlight caresses the water;
its rippling flow makes music.
I hear your voice raised in song.
I will set out to find you.

What Was He Doing

I saw a squirrel
in a pose of prayer
his nose pointing in the air
his paws together under his nose
what he was doing, nobody knows
but he taught me something
I didn't know
to see life's mysteries
as I go.

<187>

Native American

My son tells me
he sees him come
each night
to our patio.
His approach, forceful —
this is his territory.

He hungrily takes
the bread we have
set out under the oak tree —
wedge-shaped face
glittering eyes
hairless tail
a tender pink.

I have never seen him.
All I know of him
is the empty place
in the morning.
Like a reproach
to be appeased
it must be filled nightly.

And
our conscience
is eased
because
we have
taken away
everything.

*This poem has been alternately titled "'Possum," and
variations of it have been published.*

<188>

Day Turns
To Night

Morning

Trees cast long shadows
on the grass.
A filigree of light
and shade.
Over all — silence.

The only movement
one early squirrel
among the autumn leaves.

In the trees a mourning
dove calls.
A lament for the passing
beauty of nature.

Her lament
moves me to tears.

<191>

Lament

Shadows of trees
long shadows
the grass a filigree
of light and shade.
Over all, dark silence
a lone butterfly
the only movement
flits its way across
the pristine lawns.
Shallow stream
winds its way
through the woods.
In the trees a lone
mourning dove calls
a lament for beautiful
tree-bearing nature
assaulted by the enemy —
man.

An earlier version of the poem titled "Morning."

<192>

The Wind in the Trees

A secretive whispering
leaves trembling
movement like reeds under water
a soft soughing
branches waving
each leaf dancing
green with a gold patina
from the early morning sun
leaves silhouetted against gray walls
rush of sound
sudden rush of air
and this perpetual dancing
a sound like the flow of waters
from behind a cloud the sun's
gold light floods the woods

<193>

Flashes

Red houses among the trees
flashes of traffic on
the highway
the slow rise of the
hill
topped by trees
and the red brick
houses

in the distance the
soft blue of the
Kittatinnies
all shining under a
midday sun
below me the
manicured lawns of
the high rise
flowers
the roads curving
from the windows
flashes of silver.

<194>

Three Haiku

Sun behind dark clouds
A hushed expectancy
Quiet before rainfall

A whisper of wind
Frail pink cherry blossoms drift
Past open windows

When the storm passes
Brave blue colors the sky
My heart rejoices

<195>

The Day Is a Pool in a Future Forest

I
Enter in with hope
soothed by the whisper of leaves
The cries of the lost souls forgotten
All seems transcendent
Glimpses of azure sky
Uplift the mind
The trees are sentinels
At the heart of the vernal woods
The pool ripples softly
Like the beat of a tender heart.

II
The evening fox
a small impetuous King wants war:
as was ever thus
peace is an illusion
like the rare green light
at the setting of the sun.

<196>

Encounter

I go into the forest —
Leaves wink in the breeze,
A gust from the sea,
Plays a canto in the trees.
I stand silent,
God is here.

Sky

The evening sky like a comforting shawl
covers the hills
in consolation
at the close of day.

<197>

At Night

At night
the woods are silent
only the gentle fall
of leaves

the woods are asleep

Streetscape

Windows reflecting evening light
The store iron etched in gold
Open doors on empty rooms
and an echo of a voice
a whispering
a sound of whispering
the wind in the trees
and dying footsteps in the street
outside

<198>

Night

I'm told that
Austin has artificial moonlight.
Who knows night anymore?
That great stillness
under the arched heavens
filled with stars,
on clear nights
the planets blazing
the bark of a dog, distant —
and the calling of the train at Leonia
as it crosses Fort Lee Road
and clacks along by the silent park
where only the shapes of Canada geese
are shadows on the water.

You have to seek night out
mostly north, in the Maine woods
or at Walden, where the lapping lake
reflects the flinty stars.

<199>

The Moon Is Our Companion

You said "the moon
is our companion"
I looked at the sky
last night
the moon above the hemlocks
a silver disc in a deep blue sky.

I looked up at its sad face
high above us humans
and our awful follies,
shining its goodness down on us
high in the winter sky.

I remembered in Ireland
they said "When you see the new moon
make a wish."
I would watch the moon
shine her radiance down on us
paint the leaves of the trees silver

as I watch a thin skein of geese
fly slowly southwards
across the face of the moon.

<200>

The Conspiracy
Of Seasons

Conspiracy

It's April and I'm waiting
for the high-rise to disappear
behind the sweet gums.
They let me imagine
I'm in a country place
far from urban monstrosities,
nearer to the ultimate essence
of Mother Earth.

I watch these trees,
sentinels of promise
now sprouting leaves all over,
softening the rigid outlines
of buildings that do not
uplift the spirit.
Partners in a conspiracy
of imagination,
urban monoliths will vanish
until leaf fall in October.

<203>

Broken Blossoms

The quiet pool
Mirrors pink azaleas.
From the West the sound
Of distant thunder.
Raindrops mist the water,
Reflections shatter.

Before the Storm

I watch the sky above the high rises
ominous gray clouds
leaves of trees flutter
birds fly west before the storm
the streets are empty
Home is the place to be

<204>

Come Tonight

Just when I thought
"Tomorrow I will water
my garden"
this happens.
I imagine the roots in
the dry soil
as the moisture sinks
into the earth
And I remember how
it was, as a child
or ailing —
how the cooling glass
the glass of fresh water
was a holy sacrament
to be drunk to her
last drop as though
I'd never tasted
water before.

From the open window
I stretch my hand
palm up into
falling rain
like little drum taps
Each drop lands on my palm
I walk to the table
where the yellow shaded
lamp casts its golden glow
hold my hand
under its golden glow
the myriad drops
sparkle on my hand
gather in peaked clusters
wonderful that such
infinitely small droplets
millions of these small droplets
refresh the earth

<205>

Rain

I hear the rain
singing on the roof tiles,
droplets coursing
down the window panes.

Just when I thought
"Tomorrow I'll have to
water the garden"
this miracle happens.

I imagine roots
in the dry soil,
slowly revived, fortified
the thirsty grass
refreshed.

From the window
I hold my hand
into the falling rain,
each drop taps my palm,
a gentle caress.

At the table
where the lamp casts
its golden glow,
the drops on my hand
glisten in pearled clusters.

In the kitchen I pour
a glass of water
and drink it to the last drop
as though I'd never
tasted water before.

<206>

Go Slowly Through My Garden

Go slowly through my garden —
It's pretty here, you know —
It repays your efforts
To make your footsteps slow.

Linger by my fountain —
Hear the water flow—
Listen to my leafy trees
As the south winds blow.

Budtime

Buds
tender as babies' thumbs
push up
from rain-drenched earth;
in the hedge a robin sings.
I rake, winter passes
out of reach.
On the breeze
there is the scent
of the sea.

Violets

A blue shawl of violets
By the little pond
Reflecting the paler blue above

<207>

Daffodils

In my garden every Spring
Comes the gold rush of daffodils
Resisting the sometimes chilly breeze

As the days warm, their gold heads
Shine in the sun, symbols of the season
Of hope and expectation of summer.

As the days pass we cut the crowns
Of these golden visitors for our tables
When their fresh yellow cups
Cheer us out of our winter blues.

In Autumn my father cut their faded stems
Pressed, with gloved hands, the soil around them.
Stood back and smiled
Thinking of spring.

<208>

8th May 2003

It is very still —
no traffic on the street
spring foliage drenched
by last night's rain.
Blooms on the flowering cherry
show their pink faces
at the window.
Gold forsythia blossoms gleam.
Slight wind from the west
stirs the tops of trees.

I have read a poem
about just such a day.
Up the Hudson north of here
a poet watches a hare
slowly nibbling little shoots
in his windswept garden.
The animal savors
pieces of spring leaves
in a world which is past.
It does not question its meaning.

Would that I were the same —
simply accepting,
not always looking back
or filled with concern for future times —
just doing well with the necessities
and living each day well.

<209>

Patterns

The weather people
tell us
this year's summer
will be warm and
rainless.

I look out at the
pattern of tree branches
against a pale sky
and know, on days
when the air is dry
and the great orb
blazes,
I will long for
the bare trees
the damp, sweet earth
and the great arches
and structure
of the trees.

<210>

July

On this July day I look up
At the sky, a wide blanket of gray
A soft and cool expanse
And rain clouds on the way.

This sky oppresses me.
I see it filled with rain.
All hopes for warmth and sun
I cherish now in vain.

<211>

Summer Heat

This heat weighs on me.
There's no mercy
in the eye of the sun.
It tans the land,
buildings glitter like granite,
mica-flecked.
Gray haze obscures the horizon.

Roses burn with color,
no birds call.
All is silenced by the weight
of summer heat.
In the night sky
pink from city lights
no stars shine,
even the comforting darkness
has vanished.

I lie consumed by thoughts
of black holes,
greenhouse effect.
At dawn a mourning dove
tremulously calls.
A little breeze stirs
the cotton curtains.
I fall into uneasy sleep.

<212>

Storm

The highest branches of the trees
were like banners
heralding the oncoming rush of wind.
A distant sound of thunder
over all a gloominess,
a strange cold gray.

My cat looks anxious.
I switch on the light
to comfort him
but the heavy rumbling continues
like the sound of distant battle.

A police siren sounds on the highway.
There is overall a hushed expectancy.
As before, the wind strengthens, blows music
from my garden chimes.
How faint they sound beneath.

I want the storm to come
the clouds to break into war.
After an hour's grumbling,
it came to nothing —
sullen sounds
moves away to the north
still rumbling away
disgruntled.

<213>

After Rain

The sky
brightens
brave blue
unfolds
like a flag —
a sunray
pierces
the clouds
a radiant bow
arches
over the treetops.
The earth
smells
like
wine.

<214>

August

The sun comes up
yellow disc that tans the land,
gray haze obscures the horizon.
On the wires
mourning doves tremulously call,
roses burn with color.

Nights, music from a neighbor's window
punctuates the silence,
city lights pink the darkened sky.
For the tired
sleep comes towards morning
when cotton curtains gently move
in a little breeze.

<215>

Mourning Dove in August

August is here now
Half the summer is gone
Already the sky has a
Look of cooler weather —
In the trees nearby
a mourning dove coos
there is that sad subdued
look to the sky
I think of old days
when we were young
I didn't think so much
then
of time passing —
there seemed no end
to time then
now I measure the days
they seem to flee
into the past —
they seem sad —
like the dove's call

<216>

Late September

Summer is leaving
there's a sadness in the air.
Today I found leaves,
yellow of autumn
under the old maple.
It's time to say goodbye
to the long evenings.
Already the western light
is lower
our rooms on that side
of our house
grow dark earlier.

<217>

The Clear Light of Late Afternoon

Summer has gone now
the bloom is off the roses
scarlet berries sprinkle the ground
I hear the Canadas
fly south —

It's a little sad, this season
of the turning of the leaf
the tail of the hurricane
has just passed through
its as if it blew away
those lazy summer days —

the sky now is paler

small warblers flit about
in the arms of the oak trees
the voices of children seem
distant now
it's as if sound is muted
the great wheel of the sun
shines softer on the earth
readying for the winter sleep

<218>

Autumnal

Look at the field
going up to the trees
here in the autumn air.
Look at the mountain
blue beyond,
and the trembling willow's hair.

Look at the sky, a faded blue
when the last birds gather to fly
and marvel how all falls into place
when the year decides to die.

If only we could experience
this gentle letting go
and resign ourselves
to our certain end,
and do not question why,
and do not question why.

<219>

Lear Jet

Sometimes a small Lear jet
races up through the gold
autumn air into the blue sky
a white dart.

It thrills me to watch it
swiftly disappear
the tear of its engines
shredding the silence

Sunflowers

heads bowed
greeting waiting
autumn
season
leaves limp
and ragged
sleeves of an
old coat ready

<220>

October 1st 1998

Lord, today was very fine —
the leaves are turning
on the dogwood in my yard
red orange, gold, bronze
gilded by sunshine

Not the sunshine
of a month ago
now a lambent sun
that casts a gold shadow
on the grass.

Today the sky was
that shade of blue
that Rilke meant
when he wrote of a
child's pinafore.

Something soft and
tender in the blue
and something sad, too —
summer has gone now.

This most exquisite
of seasons begins
with leaves like Joseph's
many-colored cloak,
and a soft distance
in the blue haze.

<221>

Villanelle

Walking in the cemetery today
I noticed Autumn's colors on the trees
Signals of the season on the way

Over the Ramapos the sky was gray
Distant birdsong on a gentle breeze
Walking in the cemetery today

Soon I'll see the Autumn's full display
Across the valley and the far-off fields
Signals of the season on the way

The reds, the orange-yellows in array
Tease my eyes and set my heart at ease
Walking in the cemetery today

I do not feel in any sense dismay
I know that Summer's sun to Autumn yields
Walking in the cemetery today
Signals of the season on the way

<222>

The Holiness of Fall

Yesterday
a machine
in the park
roared like a lion.
Leaves, amber
gold and red,
fed into its maw.

Years ago
a few men
with a cart
slowly raked
summer's relics
from the grass —
then
it was an art
to clear the park,
a ceremony.

Voices carried
on the still air —
jokes —
a snatch of song —
it seemed fitting
and belonged
to the season.

Now
this monster
does it all —
it desecrates
the holiness
of Fall.

<223>

Autumn Evening (November)

It is that hour of evening
when the light
drifts through the trees
and turns the last leaves bright.

Darting starlings
cross the sky
in winnowed flocks
seagulls give their last lamenting cry.

In a long, slow fugue
the waning day
clouds the pale sky
in sere and fragile grey.

Over the trees, now black
against a frigid blue
the farthest clouds
reflect dazzling hue.

Haunting the west
a strip of yellow light,
in the cold east, Venus,
a single winking star, is bright.

The wheel has turned full circle
and the darkening east
holds a thin moon
tip-tilted where the clouds are least.

So ends the evening
and the stars are bright,
and in the west the thinnest line
where day has turned to night.

<224>

Autumn's Fire

I look around, see the riot of color
Standing at the edge of the forest
Unfolding before me
Trees majestic as kings and queens
In ceremonious attire
Blazing away Autumn's fire.

Autumn Glory

On my neighbor's lawn
a red tree blazes
in autumn sunshine.
It is glorious and also sad.
It is the death
of this year's leaves
and a reminder
nothing really lasts.

<225>

Before the Cold Descends

Before the cold descends
and the days end in early
darkness —
when the last of familiar birds
start to fly south
I wander in the golden woods.

Autumn To Winter

It was later when the Autumn went
Than when the swallows fled.
I felt the gentle Zephyr blow
That soon would turn to strength.

It was sooner when the winter came
Than when the wind turned cold.
And all that fearsome energy
So many secrets told.

<226>

Unease

First storm of the season —
November's dull gold and faded green.
Pigeons scatter on the rooftops,
hurled through the sky
by this windy weather.

A swaying of trees
like weeds ravaged in running water.
On bare twigs the sparrows
sit silent like
little wet mops.

The air is filled with turbulence,
the disturbing weather
relentlessly saying
It's gone, it's over
One more autumn gone, gone.

The wind roars around the house.
I sit inside in wonder.

<227>

Fireside

Outside the summer
seasons are sleeping
somewhere
and winter roars on
the hills.
We feel safe, secure
draw closer to the
fire
our winter comfort.
We tell each other tales
reminisce about
the past
turn over memories
like pages of a picture book
laughing together
sometimes we hardly
know why.
A coziness descends on us.
We add a few more
coals to the fire;
now as long as it
burns we will not
go to bed.

Look back over fifty years.
Watch the dying fire
the last glowing embers
the final comforting
flame — rose-gold
leap up —
then all are ashes.
We leave the
warm room and
go slowly to bed
as the air in the room
slowly ices.

<228>

Evocation

When I hear the
tinkle of that music box
it's winter
I see the white horses
in the bay
and the Irish Sea.

The great waves
crash over the stone pier
three miles away from
my old home
around whose walls
the wind whirls.

It's nothing to the
whirling in my ear
of lost voices, lost sounds.
Only the music box
sounds the same,
as evocative as
Proust's Madeleine.

One turn of the handle
and that old, tinny tune
brings back wintry days
along the Irish Sea.

<229>

Snow in Winter

And the snow comes
concealing
veiling the hills and
the valley
falling on Francis
Grady's stone tomb
gently laying a
fresh carpet
on the quiet earth
and on me — a special
benediction
a quiet and hushed
acceptance
as soft as the gently falling
snow.
All will be well
in its season's falling
on the quiet earth
muting the sounds
of life in the valley
like a blessing
a confirmation of the
ordered scheme of
things.

<230>

Winter Landscape

How firmly etched the trees
against the sky.

Cold clouds ride the sky.

A single bird sits pensive
in a tree.

Reflections

The trees are finely etched against the sky,
Cold clouds ride high,
A single bird sits pensive in a tree,
And all is quiet in winter harmony.

If I could capture such serenity
From Nature's source;
Such mellow peace, such glorious equanimity,
Calm Nature would reflect her mood in me.

This is an earlier version of the poem titled "Winter Landscape."

<231>

Snowfall

Walking in the falling snow
another world takes hold,
one becomes aware of silence.
Slowly, one begins to feel
the helplessness of man in Nature.
All we can do, all we have achieved
is as nothing.

Before this relentless falling
laying a white blanket
that changes everything,
snow causes one to shiver
at its compacted coldness.
The only color the sky
a hard and brilliant blue
and an east wind
mocking man's efforts
to struggle through.

<232>

Firs in Snow

Listening to the easy wind
in the fir trees
above Quabbin
I hear Earth's music
and it breaks my heart.

In the Quiet Falling

A voice speaks to me
in the quiet falling of the snow.
Tells me "Be still and listen."
This voice is from my heart.
No intellectual response
can bridge the gap
between the longing
for certitudes and
the need to know.
It is as delicate
and lovely as the falling snow.

<233>

Release

When I cease to weep
if it is winter
I hear the sweep
of wind in trees —
I try to think
quite soon, their leaves
in spring will flutter
in the breeze
and I will find
in nature an ease
from suffering.

<234>

The American Dead

I come here to honor
the dead generations
when the snow comes
veiling the valley
and the distant hills,
frosts the granite stones,
shuts out all sounds.
In the hushed stillness
of winter,
peace seems to flow upwards
from this hallowed ground.

They sleep in orderly rows
under a coverlet of snow.
At each grave a stone
gives a name and date,
nothing of the fate
that brought them here.

I think of the drama
that is America.
Four hundred years
of ocean crossings,
of struggle, hope and prayer.
All now transcended
by our common destiny.

In our modern age
this quiet disturbs
the great mystery
that surrounds
our final departure.

<235>

Winter Gothic

Now is the time
to observe the architecture
of trees,
angled and triangled
against a sky
the cold blue of winter.

More beautiful
than Baroque cathedrals
or spires of Gothic churches,
they seem to implore us,
"Raise your eyes
away from earth-bound things."

I turn to the trees,
ponder the mystery
of death and regeneration,
the dormant buds
sleeping through winter,
tentacles of roots
concealed in the earth,
like the hidden longings
of the human heart.

<236>

Advent

The wheel is turning,
turning.
We are entering the dark time
of the year.
But there is a hushed
expectancy
when we listen in silence.

Do we hear in the distance
a faint bell
heralding the Child
who entered into history
and changed, changed
life utterly?

<237>

January Morning

The sound of your shovel
Breaks the silence
Of this January morning
My hopes are dashed —
No going off now
To enjoy the day.

I stand at the window
Watching your head
Bobbing as you work
The pile of snow beside you
Growing as you dig
Spadeful after spadeful.

Digging is exercise
You tell me —
Keep the blood flowing
Good for the heart.
I watch your busy arms
and wish I were as smart.

<238>

February's Chill

If, when I looked
at the ceiling fans
that kept this room
in summer cool
I feel dismayed
at February's chill
that sometimes gives
a sense of doom.

It would not be too much to bear.
It would be too small a flaw
to shiver in my winter clothes
if I could in my thoughts as well
imagine summer's warmer days
ringing me her golden bell.

<239>

What's Happened with the Weather?

The four seasons
were once a given —
winter blew away in February
then came the March days,
still with a nip in the air
but here and there, an early violet.
Spring arrived, fresh and welcoming
blue skies and sometimes showers
and the first children played in the park.
By May all the flowers shone out
in loamy beds;
by June summer had arrived.
Our autumn days came in a haze
of reds, yellows, and golds
and ended in the mists of November.
Now we have total confusion.
What's happened with the weather?

<240>

Variations
On a Theme

Dún Laoghaire (2010 Version)

That summer morning
I watched the cormorants
on the rocks along the shore
of Dublin Bay.

Wings outstretched to dry
they faced the sea,
moving gently
from side to side.
The water, to the far horizon,
a cool and distant blue.

They moved their angled wings
with the studied gestures
of Tai Chi devotees,
stretching and bending
as if to music,
in harmony with the rippling waves.

As the sun rose higher
they turned to its thin warmth,
their dark shapes
greeting daybreak.
Then, one by one they dived
into the long fingers of sunlight
stroking the whispering sea,
and swam, heads tilted upwards
to greet the rising sun.

<243>

Killiney (2010 Version)

Walking on these hills
high above the Irish Sea
what happiness I feel
just as I felt
long ago.

I grew up here;
this was my world once.
Most are gone who knew me then.
I am a visitor
from a far country.

Below me I hear the waves
breaking on the far shore
just as I remember,
an aqueous clock
underscoring time.

Down in the bay
the flashing leap of porpoises.
I think of the old man
gazing out to sea
remembering his drowned son.

Among the pines pierced by sunlight,
cool shadows make a dim radiance
on the carpet of pine needles.
Each step releases
their spicy scent.

At the old stone wall
above the rocky quarries
blackberry and valerian still bloom.
Scented yellow gorse
stabs the air.

<244>

A soft mist rolls
in from the sea.
Soon the hills and valley
will be covered
with a pall of gray.

Evening falls
on the distant headland.
A familiar light winks —
the Kish light,[1]
guardian of the bay.

Wind rises from the sea.
Wisps of mist curdle among the trees.
The birds are silent. The foghorn sounds
haunting   evocative
begin to moan.

---

[1] *Kish light*. A lighthouse in Dublin Bay.

<245>

Merdon (1980 Version, First or Early Draft)

How well I remember Merdon
The weathering there was
On that windy hillside
Over the surging Irish Sea.
Some days, in this other climate
The wind blowing from the south,
Or the high calling of Canada geese
In the scarlet autumn,
Quickens my memory
And I recall the seasons at Merdon.

On some March days then, soft winds
Blew from the south and carried
The scent of pine forests in the Wicklow Hills.
This promise of soft weather stayed unfulfilled
When once again east winds blustered in the trees.
With the fierce equinoctial gales
The rain lashed window panes
Reflected broken light from a stormy sky,
And the hills echoed a sea bird's cry.

In summer, in the sparkling air,
Daisies starred the meadows.
Swifts swooped and swerved about the ivied eaves
And pink roses and the leaves
Of lilac, laburnum and fuchsia were tender in the sun.
On warm August nights a white moon
Silvered the little castle on the hill.
In the meadow behind the granite wall
The secretive corncrake called.

<246>

Autumn, purple asters graced the flower beds
And bronze chrysanthemums and Michaelmas daisies.
Mornings we gathered mushrooms on the hill,
Late tomatoes ripened on the window-sill,
The tang of burning leaves was in the air.
Wild geese flew southward under a hunter's moon,
A chill came in the rooms
Foretelling winter and the passing days —
The evening light died sadly down the sky.

In winter's chill, under a wan sun,
The pine trees swayed in a north wind.
On frosty days I recall the rimed grass,
My father tapped the old glass
In the dark hallway and forecast a shower of hail —
The spumy sea raced in the bay,
Grey waves crashed against the grey sea well,
The foghorns warned all through the night,
Wind in the chimney made a lonesome wailing sound.

Merdon, how lightly I left you in my youthful days —
How many times in this other climate
I am reminded of the passing of the seasons there,
Sometimes the windy weather
Is the catalyst,
Sometimes scudding clouds against an autumn moon.
You haunt me, as an old song heard in childhood
Has power to move me after years and years.

<247>

The Lost Wood (Early Version)

It was lovely the wood, and so old
Remembering its companionable trees
Where the murmuring pigeons lulled the days
The harmonious bees hummed in the hedges
It was my sanctuary and solace in these years of war

Near the stony hills, the wood,
hidden in an old demesne,
was mine, not through endowment
but through love, because I made it so
You were my first love

The seasons were canticles
the glory of the whins in autumn
Gold cups sanctified by the sun
their musky scents like forgotten sachets
in my old dresser drawer

In spring ancient branches windblown
whispered like a slow receding tide
a blue shawl of violets, enchantment in the grass
Flutes of birdsong chorused
in the greening glades

Stormy winter nights, moonlight
flooded the aisles of the trees
with pure magic
the fox barked at the moon
and the elms roared in the wind

Marvelous was the dark pool
The color of sapphires reflecting summer skies
In winter black as onyx, black as the crows
storm tossed, whose cawing filled the air
as though angry with the cold wind

<248>

One cold spring day
an old man from the village
blue eyes fierce with anger
told me the story
the wood was cut for timber

The fox homeless, the pigeons routed
the scent of whins and violets
blown on the wind, forever lost
a wood that had graced the land
for a thousand years
the hallowed land destroyed
Nothing could have saved the wood
All I had was love
and love was powerless
I am still moved to tears.

<249>

Grosse Île (2010 Version)

Quebec, Canada

A summer rain dapples the St. Lawrence,
faint cries of river birds
break the silence,
the Laurentians,
brooding, gigantic,
loom on the northern shore.

Grosse Île lies
downstream from Quebec.
Its wooded shores fret by water,
pines bend inland
by withering winter winds,
its highest point crowned
by a Celtic cross.

I come to Grosse Île,
pay homage to the Irish
sent across the Atlantic
in the coffin ships
forgotten and unwanted,
their hopes flickering
like dying fires.

That summer of 1847[2]
ships sailed up the river,
sometimes forty in a line
to the small island,
grass pink with mallow,
loosestrife purple in the green.

---

[2] Fleeing the famine in Ireland, many immigrants died on route, or were so weak
and ill they did not long survive the sea passage.

<250>

The wind sighs in the pine trees,
river birds cry distantly.
I wander along the leafy paths,
think about the thousands
who died of cholera, typhus,
in this small place.
The only evidence that they lived,
five white crosses
in the Silent Valley.

<251>

Seeking the Ancestor

The only sounds
the hiss of the gas fire
a ticking clock
and a soft wind
sighing outside the window.

In dusty ledgers
piled on a table
we try to read
faded writing
two hundred years old.

The same names
repeated over and over
like an incantation
invoke us to remembrance
a distant echo of family.

Nothing binds me to them
except a blood line.
Who were these souls
lives like a whisper
on the wind?

They lived in another country,
spoke Irish, farmed the land.
I do not know what
we are seeking.
Hard to find my own past.

<252>

At the Grave of Mary Higgins Keefe (2010 Version)

The football season has begun
in Halder, Wisconsin.

We visited the old cemetery
near the quietly flowing Wisconsin River.
In a quiet corner under pine trees
my son and I find you
"Mary Keefe born 1818 Ireland."

I place my hand against the cold granite.
Are you great Aunt Mary's marker?

<253>

Patrick Kavanagh on Pembroke Road
(2010 Version)[3]

April on Pembroke Road,
showers soak long gardens,
daffodils light dark corners.
The sky is filled with promises.

Midday, the poet, solitary man,
plods up the street
on the way to McDaids
to dispense homespun wisdom
to the lunchtime crowd.

His countryman's shoes
strike echoes from the pavement.
Arms folded on his chest,
old felt hat battened on his head,
lost in thought, he walks alone.

An outsider in urban exile,
far from the lanes of Inniskeen,
lonely as an old crow,
his days are lived
on the edge of poverty.

Hungry for female company
he greets the indifferent typist
on her way to lunch
at the Landsdowne Hotel.
She spurns his greeting.

No matter.
He trudges on to his Parnassus,
the banks of the Grand Canal
where he sees the apologetic swan
and dreams its exaltation.

---

[3] *Patrick Kavanagh* (1904-1967). Irish poet and novelist, author of *The Great Hunger.*

<254>

Upstate (2000 Version)

They were line dancing
at the inn that night
near the falls of the Sugar River.

They were all locals;
their faces glowed
in the firelit room.
Young and old
they got along famously.

I can still hear the sound
of their feet
tapping to the beat
of country music.
The air smelled
of wood smoke.

Outside, a sudden dash of rain
left Main Street glistening
in the lamplight.
Red and gold leaves
patterned the pavement.
The white gazebo was ghostlike
on the village green.

Nothing spectacular up there —
open country,
fields stripped of harvest,
rivers running cold
from the mountains.

I don't know how to explain it.
I only know
that's how it was
one October evening —
folks enjoying life together
in a small town
West of the Adirondacks.

<255>

Upstate (Later Published Version)

This town is old and small,
bounded by open country.
Fields stripped of harvest,
forests ablaze with color.
In the air the scent of wood smoke.

On Main Street scarlet leaves
scatter to the pavements,
rustle softly in the white gazebo
on the village green.
A distant sound of music —
they're line dancing
at the inn tonight.

They circle and turn
in the big old room.
Filled with quiet confidence,
they celebrate community.
Dusk closes in on the town.
Footsteps resonate
in the silence.

Nothing spectacular.
Lives in harmony with the seasons,
here the center holds.
That's how it is, this October evening,
a small town near the Sugar River,
west of the Adirondacks.

<256>

The Farm at Derry (1989 Version)

Frost's old farm
stands by a winding road.
Under the trees Hyla Brook
whispers over stones.
It is fall in New Hampshire;
the house is closed.
Through a window
I see furniture of the period,
a few books on a table,
silent empty rooms.
A barren field
girdled by walls of stone
stretches to the woods.
The field is bound by markers
to prompt memory.
There is a cemetery tidiness here.
Frost's farm is now
a place of interest
in a Mobil Guide —
there is no trace of him
at Derry.
I turn to leave.
In a sheltered corner
I see a last few Bluets —
I pick them remembering
"The Tuft of Flowers."

<257>

The Farm at Derry, N.H. 1991

Frost's old farm
stands by a winding road.
Under the trees
blazing with color
Hyla Brook whispers.
There is no other sound.

Bounded by markers
to prompt memory,
the empty pasture
girdled by walls of stone
stretches to the woods.

The house is closed.
Through a window
I see an old lamp,
a few books on a table.
Frost's farm is now
a place of reference
in a Mobil Guide.
There is no trace of him
at Derry.

In the dooryard I see
a last few Bluets.
I pick them and remember
"The Tuft of Flowers."

<258>

The Farm at Derry (2010 Version)

Frost's New Hampshire farm —
here the poet was young
fed chickens, milked cows,
dreamed dreams, where
children's voices echoed in the
apple orchard, the wild garden.

It is fall in New Hampshire.
Frost's New Hampshire farm
stands by a winding road.
Nearby Hyla Brook continues
to whisper among the stones.

The house is closed.
Through a window
I see furniture of the period,
a few books on a table,
silent empty rooms.

A barren field
girdled by walls of stones
stretches to the woods.
The field is bound by
markers to prompt memory.
There is a cemetery tidiness here.

Frost's farm is now
a place of reference
in a Mobil Guide.
There is no trace of him
in Derry.

I turn to leave.
In a sheltered corner
I see a last few Bluets.
I pick them, remembering
"The Tuft of Flowers."

<259>

Overpeck (1999 Version)

I came from the playing field
through a screen of trees
to the edge of the creek.
I had escaped to solitude.
Four Canadas sailed companionably
on the still blue water.
From the distant shore
hurrying towards me, a pen swan,
wings extended, long neck
outstretched.
What did I mean to her
standing there in the autumn
sunshine?
She stayed below me, paddling,
her big, dark feet ruffling
the water.

<260>

Hearing Brodsky Read, Dublin 1992 (2005 Version)

His voice resonating
through the prim
Protestant church
the poet declaims,
forgets,
strikes his forehead,
apologizes.

He explains
that translation
does not always work.
Heatedly
he struggles with words,
never enough to express
his emotion.

The resonant baritone
soars to the rafters.
Attentive Dubliners,
books in hand,
read the unfamiliar meters,
try to comprehend
such impassioned speech.

Their faces seem a mix
of sympathy
and bemusement.
Outside, summer swallows
swoop over the rooftops,
their distant cries
a lively
counterpoint.

<261>

Courtesy (2010 Version)

Seton Hall, March 1992, West Orange, NJ

That evening the poets
lauded Whitman
in learned, witty phrases.
In the auditorium
laughter rose and fell.
The old poet, dead
one hundred years,
would have gently smiled.

After the ceremony
and the applause,
the crowd drifted
into another space
made for conviviality.
Wine glasses clinked.
Conversation flowed.
I knew no one there.

Alone by a window,
glass in hand,
I watched the rain fall
onto a little lawn.
A small man with kind eyes
stood beside me.
We looked out together
at the vernal lawn.

Smiling, he said, "Do you know
what Whitman called grass?"
I shook my head.
"The handkerchief of the Lord.
Isn't that a beautiful thought?"
he replied, then recited:
"A child said, 'What is the grass?'
fetching in to me with full hands."[4]

---

[4] Walt Whitman, "Song of Myself," ll 99-100.

We talked of Whitman
and the shining grass.
After some time,
I ventured to ask
"What is your name?"
"Merrill, James. A poet,"
he said, and bowed,
then left to join the festive crowd.

<263>

Closing Remarks

Time, That Inexorable Thief

My thoughts turn to what is
to come —
days when I can't walk
the length of the Boulevard
when I'm hemmed in
by inclement weather
and the windows, firmly closed,
make my house a fortress
against the steel-cold air.

An air of hushed expectancy.
Only the crows call
in early morning.
I walk on the narrow
path in my garden —
it's bittersweet — this
ending of the sun season —
I try not to think
of how much time there
is left —
to write poems, to see
my friends, to visit the
distant island —
I wait for the inexorable
thief.

Nearby someone is plucking
sad notes on a piano.
They are a threnody
for the end of summer
in the failing light.

<267>

Horizon

If we could see that far
we would know where we are
not just where we are heading.

We just get a glimpse of it
occasionally
when we wander alone
in a wood
on the wide fields.

The horizon limits our sight —
our thoughts and conjectures
are just that.
We simply have to imagine
how things will be —
somehow like here
when we are in one evening
the sun slants through
the trees of the wood
and we are alone
and in the silence
the sweet sound of a wood bird singing
nothing we can put
into words.

<268>

Dust

It lies thick on surfaces
reminder of a slow and constant
disintegration —
the destiny of all.

In Ireland, long ago
people watched it on country roads
skirled by the wind
and talked of spirits.

It is always there —
finest of substances
under our feet,
on our fingers,
in the air we breathe.

In the Bible it is mentioned
as a beginning —
In the Bible it is mentioned
as an end.

<269>

The Old British Thing

Gentility, the old British thing
and in that Irish Spring
now the garden of that old hotel
is paved over
a parking lot — romance has
fled
all that is left remains
in the ivy-covered wall
and the fading snapshot
of
where you all stood[1]

---

[1] The Longford Arms Hotel, where the poet's parents held their wedding reception.

<270>

Reflections

What is it about mirrors?
We can't avoid looking
At our reflections
Even momentarily
In passing
As though we are always unsure
Of who and what we are.
And do we see,
In passing
Those whom we love
And those loved ones gone
Staring back at us
As though to say
As long as your reflection shows
We are all still here.

<271>

Starting with Two Lines by Billy Collins

Even if it keeps you up all night
Wash down the walls and scrub the floor[2]
Seek under all the tokens of your past.
Carefully select the images of memory
Tidily place the relics from long-gone times
Ponder over their content and form
Then box them away in the
hidden recesses of your mind.
Inspiration for a future day
when memories fill the
printed page.

---

[2] Billy Collins, "Advice to Writers," *The Apple That Astonished Paris* (1988).

<272>

Starting with a Line from Molly Peacock

Take a blank page[3]
and try to find the past
as it floats to the top of your mind
in pictures as many-colored as a
summer garden in full bloom.

Now is the time to pick and choose
those flowers, bright specimens
of early summer.
Disregard the weeds you will
now and then find.

To choose the best
and leave the rest
to healing time —
this is the course you must take
to live a life to the full.

---

[3] From the poem "Life Study" in Molly Peacock's *Original Love* (1995).

<273>

You Know, When You Think About It

I don't know what we're
going to do about all
the poor in the world.

A Window Shut to Keep Out Pain

Prompted from a line from "The Family Group"
by Madeline de Frees

How does one cope with sorrow
or, for that — the nagging worries
that interfere in life?
Daily, from early morning's reading
of the heartbreaking news
which lodges in the heart and mind
and makes us seek what one cannot
really find —
a window shut to keep out pain.

<274>

Threnody

I know the way
the light enters there —
a slanting cool shaft
on the patterned carpet

the low light of autumn
and the trees bronze
and brown
a threnody
for summer.

He said to me
"You can't go back."
I know he was right —
but it's hard
to give up this longing
to walk out again
to the road that winds up the hill
and in the distant bay
watch the sea mists
creep towards the shore
as the foghorn's sad voice
warns evocative
recalls other voices, stilled.

<275>

Shadow of a Rose

One evening a friend
brought me roses,
the old-fashioned kind,
a delicate pink.
In a glass vase,
the color of their perfect
leaves, green as emeralds.
Their scent fills my room
with nostalgia.
They remind me
of frilly skirts,
children's party dresses,
the kind we called "frocks"
long ago.
They evoke dreamy waltzes,
glasses filled
with pale lemonade,
the sound of patent leather shoes
on a parquet floor.
As they fade
something of the spirit
of a rose lingers in my room,
the way ghosts are said
to linger in places
that they love.
Their petals gently fall
on my polished table.
One remains, upright on its stem.
I pin it to my blouse.
It rises and falls
with the beat of my heart.

<276>

To Grow Old

Starting with a prompt from Donald Hall's "Affirmation"

To grow old is to attain wisdom
learn to appreciate life's small gifts
greetings of friends
affection of loved ones,
however few remain.

To grow old is to take joy in Nature's bounty
the green of spring leaves
blue skies of Spring, bird song in Summer,
even, if we are able, enjoy the snows of winter
falling like a soft shawl on the earth.

To grow old is to quietly remember
the joys of the past
and even the sorrows we have endured
and feel courageous because we have
bravely survived.

Remember

Old age is nothing.
Believe me, I know.

<277>

My Life in Seventeen Lines

Name: Moira — an ancient Scottish name
Childhood Ambition: a child longed to be a dancer
    never realized
Fondest memory: playing with three brothers
    was happiness
Soundtrack: Gershwin — Summertime
Retreat: The hills above the Irish Sea
    there I could hide from the world
Wildest dream: I longed to travel everywhere
    Africa, Asia, America.
Proudest moment: when I learned to communicate
    in another language, I felt joy.
Biggest challenge: the bane of my life, mathematics.
Alarm clock: —.
Perfect day: To hike in the woods — listen to the
birds
First job: writing about documentaries
    for Hibernia Films
Indulgence: drinking wine with friends
Last Purchase: Buying President Carter's book
Favorite Movie: too many to name
Inspiration: Father and Mother, now long gone to rest
My life: some sorrow and much joy.
My life: a happy one.

<278>

The Approach

As the river calmly approaches the waterfall
So it is with our lives — as a child
the infant is caressed and cuddled
protected by parents from turmoil and sounds.

What I took that to be
can seem like a distant roar.
Then comes youth and life's calmness
Becomes like the waves on a river
as it increases its flow.

When the river reaches the falls
the sound of rushing water increases
as it thunders over the falls.
Like my life, beginning in calmness
I am beset by haste and turmoil.
I whirl through trouble
Far removed from the past.

<279>

Longing

I empty myself of
those images
that fill my mind
and cause my nights
to be cursed
by uneasy dreams.

I make a conscious effort
to live in the present
dismiss the past
and lay loved ones to rest.
Now my nights are easy.

Nevertheless, sometime
a rainy day, an old song
recalls the past.
For a moment, my old self
reappears —
I realize, beneath all
I am the same.

<280>

Spring 2008

I came to work one sunny day
just to tend the phone.
I got three calls and then no more
I really felt alone.
Oh how I wished some (friendly call)
would

In the notebook next to this poem was a flyer for an Empire Club event in Little Ferry, NJ, dated May 14, 2008.
This is likely the start of one of Moira's more recent poems.

<281>

Pilgrimage

One foot in front of the other —
I've come this far
Sharing joys and sorrows
With those I love
Long gone ahead of me
On this pilgrimage — to what?
No one knows —
We only go on
Sometimes light of step
Sometimes trudging —
Sometimes heavy of heart
Perhaps fearing to enter the unknown
Or, if we're lucky
Believing at our destination
All will be well.

<282>

A Way to Be Remembered

It is all a mystery —
son, husband, father.
After my spirit departs this life
what of my identity
will remain in the memories
of those whose lives
entwined with mine?

Perhaps I am seeking consolation
facing the reality of death.
It is not a final "good-bye"
but, encompassed by love,
my earthly presence will live on
within the hearts of those
whose lives I touched
by kindness, love and humor,
a way to be remembered.

<283>

Measuring Time

All clocks tick off time that has passed
and gone.
This clock marks each arriving
moment, each gift of time
each second
each minute
hour and day
still to be filled.

The clock's steady ticking
marks off time for me
marks each passing moment
inexorably.

Today I resolved
to learn a new way
to measure time —
each gentle tick will henceforth
mark an arriving moment.
Each minute and each hour
a day
still to be filled.

<284>

Notes

Hopes spur you on
to take chances
to try and try again

Watching the pigeons
gathering again to be
fed.

Light at end of tunnel
Last glimmer of consciousness
Before darkness descends —

What We Leave

We leave no lasting
sign on earth
we are here and gone
like a summer breeze

Lost Treasures

Where are the little things
that unexpectedly come
into our minds, gone.

<285>

Past

Up here the past lies heavy on the heart.
There's too much of it —
old wrongs, old past injustices
crowd around
like ghosts.

Remember, remember.
Too much past is stifling.
Break free.
Forget the wrongs.
Get on with it.

What Is Truth

It is that
Canada does not
export exotic
flowers.

<286>

Imagining the Future

When I try to imagine the future,
I ask a recurring question —
what will it bring to the world I know?
Down the years change will come.
New generations will fashion
a world different from ours.

Yet, I am optimistic —
the sun will rise as always,
banishing the shadows.
Rain will fall, nourishing the earth.
The green of spring will cheer our hearts.
Folks will smile at one another,
offer help to those in need.

All depends on willing efforts.
To extend our hands to others,
in kindness and friendship,
and for all of us to strive
to preserve the beauty of nature,
God's gift to mankind.

<287>

What History Has Proven

A young man wants me
to trust that all
will be well in the end.

I tell him my fear
outweighs my faith.
History has proven otherwise.

<288>

Autumn Again

It is autumn again
a light rain
taps the window pane
the leaves are beginning
a slow death
stealthy process
and I'm sitting here
in the quiet room
like a watcher
in the death room
in the oak trees
are patches of leaves yellow
show the old gold
like my grandfather's watch
time ticks by
it is autumn again
it's the sad season
the great reminder
I'm only a whisper
on the winds of time
we are only whispers

<289>

Fir Tree

Strange,
I hardly noticed
sweet sadness in the sand
how long it took
to grow so tall!

The logs lie
heaped by the pathway—
tumbled together
around him the
sawdust yellow as
corn
the branches
a rich, heart-breaking
green
I used to listen
at night
to the sweep
and sway of
its branches
against the roof
and the rush of
the wind
a soughing and
sighing

Now that it's gone
it seems to fill
the space it
occupied for years
so that, passing
I can see it
more clearly
than when it was there.

<290>

It's the space where a thing was
that creates havoc in the mind
sooner or later
we all leave this
space
and only our imaginings
fill the space
with a whispering
a sighing —
"Here,
I was here
    here
    here."

<291>

AFTERWORD

MOIRA BAILIS is one of the few living poets in the United States to write poems in nine different decades (an achievement also made by Stanley Kunitz, who wrote between 1928 and 2006). Her earliest poem is "9 Sept 1939" (written on that date, at the age of 18), and her latest poem is "Outback" (a "found poem" culled from a 2010 conversation). These are two of the 190 poems that grace *The Antidote to Prejudice*, the first of a two-volume set of *Collected Poems of Moira Bailis*. This and the second volume, a 260-poem collection titled *It Has To Do With Seeing*, are scheduled for publication on her 90th birthday in late February 2011. Between the two volumes, over 200 never-before-seen poems will make their public debut.

The Antidote to Prejudice celebrates 75 years of travel, from her first trip at the age of 15 to her local journeys these days in the town of Fort Lee, New Jersey, where she has lived since January 1, 1966. "Travel is fatal to prejudice, bigotry, and narrowmindedness," said Mark Twain, in 1869 — a remark that retains heightened relevance today, in our world of increasing polarization, self-centeredness, righteousness, and intolerance. *It Has to Do With Seeing* clusters additional poems thematically, and also includes early and variant texts.

Moira started life in Ireland in 1921, lived in Europe in the 1950s, moved to the United States in the 1960s, and over the course of her life traveled across four continents: North America, Europe, Asia, and Australia. Poems that could be perceived as capturing the spirit or essence of South America, Africa, and even Antarctica were selected and arranged to round out Volume 1.

When anyone reaches age 90 or higher, like it or not, he or she becomes "living history." Thus, many of her poems — especially in the Ireland section — are dually interesting from the standpoints of poetic craft and the capturing of history, from "On Seeing Maud Gonne, Dublin 1942" to "The Last Tram, November 1949."

Moira crossed paths with a lot of interesting people — no surprise, considering her early background as a journalist. Some of these encounters inspired interesting poems, while some parts of her personal history were never captured in poetry (such as the time she was the personal tour guide for Ralph Ellison in Germany, shortly after publication of *Invisible Man*). Personal encounters with Maud Gonne, Patrick Kavanagh, Sheelagh Kirby, Joseph Brodsky, James Merrill, and more are among the finds within the two-volume set.

While Moira was extensively published in my publication, *Sensations Magazine*, across two decades, her work also appeared in other literary

<293>

magazines and publications both in the United States and Ireland, including *Appalachian Journal*, *Contemporary Review*, *Irish Voice*, *Journal of Irish Literature*, *Parnassus*, *Poet Magazine*, and others listed in the Publication Credits section.

Many poets hinge their careers on whom they've met and where they've published. More important to Moira, however, is the attempt to create art through poetry, to share and impart knowledge, and to find beauty — whether in a person, place, thing, or the world at large. She also doesn't shy away from outlining evil, or examining and chronicling intolerance and injustice, as poems such as *"Wir hatten uns gefürchtet..."* and "Mississippi Death Trip" strongly show.

Throughout her life, and into today, Moira would strike up a conversation with a complete stranger, and utilize that opportunity to learn about that person's language, culture, background, ideals, and dreams. Some of the poems in this collection derive from that process, and we all benefit from the results.

I chose a thematic sequencing of Moira's poetry for the two-volume set. Moira did not date many of her poems, so a straight chronological sequencing of 450 pieces written across nine decades is impossible (though I will take a stab at creating a researched chronology of her poetry in the near future). All of the poems published in her now out-of-print 2003 chapbook *poems* (ISBN 0967-6066-9-1) are republished across the two-volume set, incorporating edits that she wanted included. All of her poems previously published in magazines in the United States and Ireland are republished as well. If you purchase both volumes, 98% of her lifetime of poetry writing will be in your hands.

Moira was strongly engaged in the American poetry scene for over 20 years. She worked at her poetry, rewriting and revising frequently to get each poem to the best level she could. Unlike many American poets, she occasionally wrote in form; her efforts at haiku, acrostic, villanelle, and in meter and rhyme are among these published works.

Moira attended writing workshops offered through the Main Street Poets in Fort Lee, NJ; she also was a member of the North River Poets, the Saturday Afternoon Poets, the New Jersey Poetry Society, and the League of Minnesota Poets. She was a featured reader in many poetry series in New Jersey, reading at independent bookstores, libraries, and museums. As a wide-ranging scholar, she researched and lectured on Chinese, Irish, Jewish, and Russian poets, as well as other writers ("The Poetry of James Joyce," "Shakespeare's Irish Connection") and other topics (*e.g.*, the American Labor Movement, Sacco and Vanzetti). She co-hosted a monthly poetry radio show, "The Poet's Corner," on Sunday mornings on WFDU-FM from 1996 to 2007. As a volunteer, she taught English to Korean

<294>

students in Fort Lee and, starting in 1986, held annual children's poetry workshops at Fort Lee Public Library during National Library Week.

While researching and securing the manuscript for this book, we uncovered personal letters to her by Joseph Parisi, famed editor of *Poetry Magazine*. She also corresponded with Kathryn Stripling Byer, Poet Laureate of North Carolina (in her book, *Black Shawl*, Byer dedicates her poem "Backwater" to Moira Bailis, with thanks for information she supplied concerning early Irish culture); and with other editors and writers of note. Moira offered them her words and thoughts, and frequently received personal, nongeneric replies — a very atypical experience compared to most American writers. She also wrote 17 short stories, two of which are pubished or forthcoming in *Sensations Magazine*.

"A job well done is its own reward," Moira shrewdly observes in "Cleaning House," one of the last poems in this collection. When taking a full-blown "collected works" approach to publishing, you take a risk — not every poem is necessarily a fully polished gem, and how to handle variations upon variations of individual poems is a challenge that has vexed numerous editors across the centuries. The approach here is to publish as much as possible, and to let each reader decide which individual poems or version of poems he or she prefers. It is my hope that, more often than not, you will find a great deal of talent, achievement, insight, wisdom, and beauty in her words. I am especially pleased to share this collection with her while she too is able to see, enjoy, and appreciate it.

To me, Moira Bailis is not just a fine poet and close personal friend — she has long been an example of graciousness, egalitarianism, and sincere encouragement and support of others in the New Jersey poetry scene. I was pleased to volunteer much of my spare time in 2010 to bring this project to completion, and view this endeavor as a way of saying "thank you" — on behalf of all who have interacted with her in poetry over these many decades — for creating a series of little observations and moments that add up to a comprehensive collection that speaks volumes about the world at large.

Let the world take note — and maybe learn to add a little travel to its personal itinerary.

— *David Messineo*
Thanksgiving 2010

<295>

ABOUT MOIRA BAILIS

MOIRA BAILIS was born as "Moira Geraldine Moore" on February 26, 1921 in a large 18th Century Georgian house, in Athlone, County Westmeath, Ireland, to Andrew Moore and Gertrude Moore (*née* Higgins). As she relates in a hand-written autobiographical sketch, "It began ... In a big front bedroom in 'The Park,' Athlone, Co. Westmeath, Ireland. At that time, the Irish were fighting to get the British occupiers out of Ireland. Because of the situation, no doctor could come to my parents' house, so my mother had only the care and help of a nurse."[1] More details were gleaned from Moira by a New Jersey interviewer: "...a very pregnant mother, a nervous husband, a nurse, two servants, and two gun dogs awaited the arrival of the new baby the mother was about to deliver. As the guerillas and the British soldiers exchanged gunfire outside, the young father-to-be realized help was needed. So he broke the curfew, evaded the fighting, and walked into town to fetch the doctor. The laboring mother waited amid the sounds of guns pinging as the nearby combatants struggled. The dogs added to the uproar by whining and yowling incessantly. Young Moira's eventual arrival added just the right note of excitement."[2]

Moira was educated in private schools in Ireland. During WWII, while in Ireland, Moira spent most of her days at the Carnegie Library in Dún Laoghaire, reading and strengthening her background in literature, history, and the classics, and beginning what would become a life-long interest in self-education. She speaks five languages: English, Irish (Gaelic), German, Italian, and French.

Moira married filmmaker George Fleischmann in Dublin in 1947. In Dublin, she worked as a freelance journalist, starting with short documentary film scripts for Hibernia Films, along with articles for newspapers and magazines.

Her interest in travel took her to Switzerland and Austria in 1949 and 1950. She stayed with in-laws in Graz. Then, from 1952 to 1953, she lived in Rome, where she quickly learned Italian and, in turn, taught English to individuals.

In 1954, she lived in Cologne, Germany where, under the name "Moira Moore-Fleischmann" she was writing articles on German post-war reconstruction and other topics for the *Irish Independent* and for magazines. Moira met several writers and artists while living in Germany, including the future Nobel Prize winner Heinrich Böll. She arranged for him to visit

---

[1] Bailis, Moira. Autobiographical sketch, unpublished ms., dated June 29, 2008.
[2] Marshall, Pat. "An Irish poet in our midst!" Parishioner Profile column, *All Saints News*, Dec 1995/Jan 1996 (Leonia, NJ), p. 1.

<296>

Ireland, and in exchange, he arranged for her to have her own weekly radio show in Cologne, where she conducted journalism programs on Irish culture for *Nordwestdeutscher Rundfunk* (Northwest German Broadcasting -NWDR). One of the individuals she interviewed was the African-American novelist Ralph Ellison (*Invisible Man*). She also served as his personal tour guide during the German leg of his world tour.

In 1955 she lived in Munich, not far from a U.S. Army base ... "the most touching thing I saw were these two G.I.'s surrounded by children and they were giving the kids candy. It spoke a lot about the American character."[3]

In the summer of 1959, Moira was vacationing with her young son, Stefan, in a mountain inn near Innsbruck, Austria. The host of the inn asked Moira if she would mind being seated with an American tourist as he didn't speak German. Moira agreed. The American was a New York attorney named Jacob "Jack" Bailis. Although they soon returned to their respective homelands, they maintained a long-distance courtship. Her marriage to George Fleischmann having long faded, Moira obtained a divorce and subsequently married Jack in New York. Her family was completed with the arrival of her second son, Peter. Her marriage to Jack would be an enduring one, lasting until his sudden death in September, 2007.

Moira moved to the United States on July 15, 1963. The family lived for the next two-and-a-half years in upper Manhattan, off Broadway, adjacent to Fort Tryon Park. The park provided an opportunity for Moira to re-discover her creative talents, and she composed a number of watercolor paintings during this period.

On January 1, 1966, Moira and her family moved across the Hudson River to Fort Lee, New Jersey. At this point, she started volunteering in local schools to teach English to foreign students, before English as a Second Language courses were available. Her facility with languages enabled her to volunteer to teach English to Japanese, Greek, Hispanic, and Chinese children in Fort Lee Public School Number One.

According to another journalist, "The two things that impressed her the most in those first months were the enormous *amount* of volunteerism in America, and the awareness of the poor in America. . . . 'I was shocked that there were desperately poor people here. . . . I just wasn't prepared for the extreme poverty in Appalachia or on Indian reservations.'"[4] Moira got involved in several fronts of activism: visiting Indian reservations, joining the Quaker anti-war movement during the Vietnam war, joining the Cesar Chavez farm-worker movement (and having an opportunity to meet and

---

[3] Schmelter, Robert. "Romantic Irish spirit lives on in Moira Bailis" 'Local Poet' column, *Fort Lee Suburbanite*, April 28, 2006.

[4] Gressle, Gail. "Some things she did" in "A Gallery" column, published circa 1984.

<297>

talk with him personally), then protesting the growing nuclear threat. "She also volunteered her time and energy with the Irish Republican Club, a group that was for a non-sectarian Ireland; for the gradual development of uniting the whole of Ireland through political, social, and industrial means and not with arms."[5] Author Gail Gressle adds "I have joined hands with this 63-year-old woman to make a 'human chain for peace' across the George Washington Bridge."[6] Moira's husband Jack was a member of Lawyers' Committee on American Policy Towards Vietnam, and poems such as "Vietnam Christmas 1967," "Vietnam Christmas 1969," and "Indo-China" (June 26, 1972) stem from her impressions and experiences during that era. In 1971, Jack Bailis and the antiwar lawyers' group did a sit-in at the Capitol in Washington. He was arrested with them, and spent a night in jail, sharing his jail cell with famed child pediatrician Dr. Benjamin Spock.

While she had been an "occasional poet" since the age of eighteen, Moira focused even more of her energy into poetry and literature — and volunteer public service in those arts — starting in the 1980s. She began sending out works for publication circa 1988, and received her first notable publication credit (*Irish Voice* Poetry Contest, 2nd place in a contest with over 1,000 entries) in 1990. Several poetry awards followed in the 1990s and 2000s. Moira taught children's poetry workshops at Fort Lee Public Library starting around 1986 and for close to 20 years annually, as part of National Library Week, and also set up annual exhibits at the library on Irish culture and language around St. Patrick's Day.

Starting in the 1990s, Moira gave lectures on labor history at the Botto House/The American Labor Museum in Haledon. She also gave lectures on Irish culture and history at many places, including a class at Bergen Community College.

From 1996 to 2007, she was host of the Sunday morning radio show "The Poet's Corner" on WFDU-FM 89.1 (Fairleigh Dickinson Radio, Teaneck, NJ), sharing hosting duties with Dr. Leo Thorne (1996-circa 2001) and Okey Chenowith (circa 2002-2007). Throughout the 1990s and 2000s, she conducted poetry workshops and lectures, having "learned how to conduct poetry workshops from another writer, Lois Van Houten, ten years ago."[7] Lectures written by Moira on poets of various cultures (Chinese, Irish, Jewish, and Russian), and on individual poets (Akhmatova, Heaney, Joyce, Shakespeare, and more) have been found and documented among her papers.

Also starting in the 1990s, Moira joined several local poetry groups: The Saturday Afternoon Poets (Passaic), the North River Poets (Fort Lee),

---

[5] *Ibid.*
[6] *Ibid.*
[7] Nieves, Bianca A. "She's Devoted to Libraries." *The Bergen Record*, Wednesday, August 28, 1991. p. SE-2.

<298>

and the Main Street Poets (Fort Lee), where writing prompts by workshop leader Patrick Hammer, Jr. influenced the construction of many of the poems in this collection. She was an active member of the Bergen Poets, the New Jersey Poetry Society, the League of Minnesota Poets, and took part in many of the public and private readings held by *Sensations Magazine* from 1992 to present. Also during this decade, she began her long-term writer/editor relationships with three literary magazine publisher/editors: Melanie Pimont (*North River Review*), Carole Heffley (*Feelings Poetry Magazine*), and David Messineo (*Sensations Magazine*), all of whom have published her work prominently and frequently (the Publication Credits section in both volumes details these and other publication credits). In 2003, Moira teamed up with Ana Doina to prepare and publish *poems*, a chapbook containing 46 of Moira's poems. Moira also wrote the foreword to one published poetry book: *A Dusting of Star Fall: Love Poems* by Sal Buttaci.

A core component of Moira's life has been to help and bring attention to others, even in small ways. Moira was one of two individuals to help get a plaque installed at the homestead of writer Elizabeth Bowen in Ireland. In 2003, while taking one of her many walks through Fort Lee, she rediscovered the grave of a forgotten Civil War soldier, James Conway (subject of her poem "Hero") at Madonna Cemetery. She brought it to the attention of a local VFW post in Fort Lee, and the grave was subsequently marked and rededicated. She also supported many animal rights groups.

In a handwritten biographical note, Moira mentions that her favorite poets include Keats, Yeats, Hardy, Edward Thomas, Longfellow, Frost, Mary Oliver, Carruth, Donald Hall, Heaney, and Joan McBreen. She is frequently quoted in articles which can be found about her online, discussing her passions for libraries, books, poetry, volunteerism, and the importance of helping and supporting others, especially those in need.

Moira has two sons, Stefan and Peter, and one grandson, Jacob. Moira still resides in Fort Lee, New Jersey, in the home she and her family moved into on January 1, 1966, making her a Fort Lee resident for 45 years. She turned 90 on February 26, 2011.

<299>

PUBLICATION CREDITS — AMERICA AND IRELAND

At the end of 2010, Moira Bailis has between 200 to 225 poetry publication credits, as outlined below. She wishes to thank the editors and publishers of the following publications, past and present, for sharing her writings with their audiences during the 1990s, 2000s, and 2010s.

Editor's Note: For each listing, poems are listed in alphabetic order by title. Poems labeled "unverified at press time" may be poems submitted and published, or poems submitted but not selected for publication. This section should be viewed as a work in progress, and we welcome feedback from those who can verify any partial or missing information.

POEMS PUBLISHED IN JOURNALS, LITERARY MAGAZINES, NEWSLETTERS, AND NEWSPAPERS

Appalachian Journal (1 poem, verified)
> Volume 30, No. 1, Fall 2002, p. 124.
>> "The Museum at Cullowhee"

The Black River Journal (5 poems, all verified)
> December 2001, p. 16.
>> "Autumn Rapture"
> February/March 2002, p. 9.
>> "Hiking the Columbia Trail"
> Spring 2002, p. 23
>> "A Peaceful Place"
> Holiday/Early Winter 2002/03, p. 22.
>> "A Jersey Welcome"
> Spring/Summer 2003, p. 14.
>> "The Source"

BP Links (Quarterly Newsletter of Bergen Poets) (9 poems, 5 verified)
> Vol. 1, 1999 (unverified at press time)
>> "Oracle," "The Farm at Derry," "Upstate"
> Vol. 1, Issue 2, 1999, p. 4.
>> "The Holiness of Fall," "Mending Glass"
> Vol. 2, Issue 4, Fall 2000
>> "It Has to Do With Seeing," "Memento," "Sonas"
> 2001 (claimed/unverified at press time)
>> "Rain"

The Contemporary Review, Iowa (6 poems, all verified)
> January 2001

<300>

"It Has to Do With Seeing," "Sonas," "The Farm at Derry"
July 2001, pp. 4-6.
"Courtesy," "The Bike," "The Lions of Rome"

Dalkey Community Council Newsletter (Ireland) (4 poems, 2 verified)
1995 (unverified at press time)
"Berrying" (aka "Brambles in Ireland"), "Feral," "Heartland"
September 1995, No. 235, p. 9.
"Feral"
October 2004, No. 336, Vol. 1., p. 23.
"Autumn Rapture"

Defined Providence (1 poem, verified)
Vol. 6, 1998, p. 42.
"Upstate"

Feelings Poetry Magazine (8 poems, 6 verified)
1992 (unverified at press time)
"After Rain"
Vol. 4, No. 3, Spring 1993, p. 23.
"Rained Out Boulevard"
Vol. 5, No. 2, Winter 1993, p. 11.
"Sales Pitch"
Vol. 6, No. 1., Fall 1994, p. 34.
"Oil Eater"
Vol. 7, No. 1, Autumn 1995, p. 20.
"The Farm at Derry"
Vol. 7, No. 2, Winter 1996, p. 39.
"Winter Comfort"
Vol. 7, No. 6, p. 6.
"The Source"
Spring 1997 (unverified at press time)
"Rain"

Irish Voice (1 poem, verified)
Sat Nov 24, 1990, p. 21.
"Brambles" (aka "Brambles in Ireland")
Second Place in contest with over 1,000 entries.
Earliest known poetry publication credit.

Journal of Irish Literature (1 poem, verified)
Vol. XXII, No. 3, September 1993 (Last Issue), p. 111.
"On Seeing Maud Gonne"

<301>

The Moccasin (League of Minnesota Poets) (25 poems, all verified)
    Vol. LVII, 1994, p. 42.
        "Coming Into the Heartland By Air"
    Vol. LVIII, 1995, pp. 15 & 23.
        "August," "Broken Blossoms"
    Vol. LIX, 1996, pp. 10, 11 & 43.
        "A gentle spring breeze" (Haiku), "Rained Out Boulevard,"
            "Winter Gothic"
    Vol. LX, 1997, pp. 21 & 45.
        "Advent," "Rain"
    Vol. LXI, 1998, pp. 15 & 28.
        "He Says," "Patronymic"
    Vol. LXII, 1999, pp. 28 & 31.
        "Father" (aka "Forecast"), "Summer Heat"
    Vol. LXIII, 2000, p. 28.
        "Oil Eater"
    Vol. LXIV, 2001, pp. 26, 31 & 37.
        "Elegy for a Brother" (aka "Oracle"), "Rainstorm," "Williams
            Country" (aka "Memento")
    Vol. LXV, 2002, pp. 26 & 35.
        "Brambles in Ireland," "Diner"
    Vol. LXVI, 2003, pp. 17, 21, 27 & 35.
        "A whisper of wind" (Haiku), "Remember," "Sun behind
            dark clouds" (Haiku), "The Bike"
    Vol. LXVII, 2004, pp. 14 & 18.
        "Haiku," "Teddy"
    Vol. LXVIII, 2005, p. 34.
        "Hearing Brodsky Read, Dublin, 1992"

New Hibernia Review (8 poems, all verified)
    Vol. 9:2, Summer 2005, pp. 42-59.
        "Allta," "Burning Coal," "Company Manners," "Heartland,"
            "Memento," "The Museum at Cullowhee,"
            "Patrick Kavanagh on Pembroke Road,"
            "Three Rock Mountain"

NJ Conservation Foundation (1 poem, unverified at press time)
    1995
        "Highlands"

Nimrod (1 poem, unverified at press time)
    2001
        "Ancestors"

<302>

North River Review (35 poems, all verified)
 Issue 1, Spring 1992, pp. 8, 10, 15, 17.
  "Alone in the Cemetery," "Diner" (aka "At the Diner"),
  "Passage at Overpeck," "Stiles"
 Issue 2, Fall/Winter 1992, pp. 10, 18, 21, 25, 34.
  "Consanguinity," "For Emily Brontë," "He Says,"
  "The Holiness of Fall," "The Source"
 Issue 3, 1993, pp. 1, 4, 8, 15, 24, 28, 37.
  "Confusion," "Early Morning Encounter with the Entomologist,"
  "Just Like Jane," "Light Touch," "Medieval,"
  "Mending Glass," "Rosebud"
 Issue 4, 1994, pp. 2, 9, 17, 26, 31.
  "At the Bay," "Hearing Brodsky Read, Dublin, 1992"
  (aka "Brodsky Reads"), "Patronymic," "The Farm
  at Derry, N.H., 1991," "Wir hatten uns Gefürchtet..."
 Issue 5, 1995, pp. 3, 7, 15, 17.
  "Allta," "Miss Holybrooke in Central Park," "On Seeing
  Maud Gonne, Dublin, 1944," "Sonas"
 Issue 6, 1996, pp. 2, 8, 11.
  "Four Haiku," "In China," "Upstate"
 Issue 7, 1997, pp. 6, 27.
  "Highlands," "Masterpiece"
 Issue 8, 1998, pp. 8, 32.
  "Conspiracy," "Memento"

Parnassus Literary Journal (18 poems, 13 verified)
 1997 (unverified at press time)
  "Nice Day"
 1998 or 1999 (claimed/unverified at press time)
  "Just Like Jane"
 Vol. 22, No. 2, Summer 1998, p. 79.
  "Discretion"
 Vol. 23, No. 1, Spring 1999, p. 54.
  "After Rain"
 Vol. 23, No 3, Fall/Winter 1999, p. 27
  "A is for Aardvark"
 Vol. 24, No. 1, Spring 2000, p. 11.
  "Sol"
 Vol. 25, No. 2, Summer 2001, p. 49.
  "Lightweight, as in Superficial"
 Vol. 25, No. 3, Fall/Winter 2001, p. 31.
  "Diner" (aka "At the Diner")
 Vol. 26, No. 1, Spring 2002, p. 5

<303>

"Sales Pitch"
Vol. 26, 2003 (claimed/unverified at press time)
    "Brambles in Ireland," "Voice Mail"
Vol. 27, No. 2, Summer 2003, p. 15.
    "Poetry Class"
Vol. 27, No. 3, Fall/Winter 2003, p. 6.
    "Autumn Rapture"
Vol. 28, No. 1, Spring 2004, pp. 67-68.
    "Stiles," "The Bike"
Vol. 28, No. 2, Summer 2004, p. 73.
    "Aftermath"
Vol. 29, No. 1, Spring 2005, p. 61.
    "Where Is My Father?"
Vol. 29, No. 2, Autumn 2005, p. 31.
    "Bird and the Sea"

Poet Magazine (3 poems, 1 verified)
    Vol. 4, No. 3, Winter 1992-1993, p. 17.
        "Brambles in Ireland"
    1994 (claimed/unverified at press time)
        "Just Like Jane," "Mending Glass"

Poetry Forum Journal (5 poems, all verified)
    1991 (One of six contest winners)
        "Irish September"
    March 1993, p. 13.
    "Rosebud"
    Fall 1993, p. 15.
        "A Small Remembrance"
    1994
        "Budtime"
    Fall 1995, p. 13
        "Native" (aka "Native American")

Pralaton (1 poem, verified)
    No. 17, August 2006, pp. 21-22.
        "Just Like Jane"

Quabbin Voices: The Friends of Quabbin Newsletter (2 poems,
    both verified)
    Vol. 7, No. 4, p. 5.
        "Landfall," "Quabbin"

<304>

Sensations Magazine (30 poems, 2 stories, 1 book review, all verified)
Issue 8, Fall 1992, p. 36.
"Reds"
Issue 9, 1993, p. 44.
"Bird and the Sea"
Issue 10, Summer 1994, p. 12.
"Mississippi Death Trip
Issue 11, Winter 1994-1995, p. 53.
"Dreamers"
Issue 12, 1995, inside back cover w/full color photography.
"Mr. Meyer at Coney Island"
Issue 13, 1996, p. 29.
"French Nails"
Issue 14, Spring 1997, p. 82.
"Heritage" (also "The Atheist" — fiction by Moira Bailis)
Issue 16, Fall 1997, p. 23.
"Happiness" (aka "Sonas")
Issue 17, Winter 1997, p. 38.
"Miss Holybrooke in Central Park"
Issue 38, Spring 2005, pp. 86-87.
Critical review of *poems* by Moira Bailis (2003 chapbook).
Issue 40, 2006, p. 229 & p. 263.
"Imagining the Future," "Three Rock Mountain"
Issue 42, Fall/Winter 2007, p. 296 & p. 313.
"On Seeing Maud Gonne, Dublin, 1942" and "Sonas"
(republished in memory of Jack Bailis)
Issue 44, Fall/Winter 2008, pp. 14-15, w/full color photography.
"Dreamers" (republished from Issue 11)
Issue 46, Fall/Winter 2009, p. 30.
"In Emily's Garden"
Issue 47, Spring/Summer 2010, p. 26 & p. 70.
"Rap," "The Two Swans"
Issue 48, Fall/Winter 2010, p. 24, 41, 45, 64 & 67.
"Aftermath," "August 2005 - Riegelsville, PA," "In the Republic
of Caring," "Sol," "Summer Heat"
Sensations Magazine Supplement 3, "American Presidents,"
Spring 2011
"JFK"
Sensations Magazine Silver Anniversary Fiction Issue 49,
Winter 2011,accepted/publication coming.
"A Fearful Child" (fiction)
Sensations Magazine Silver Anniversary Poetry Issue 49,
Winter 2011, accepted/publication coming.

<305>

"A House with No Key," "Alignment," "Antietam,"
   "Autumn Again," "Coming from Fort Worth,"
   "Wir hatten uns Gefürchtet..."
Sensations Magazine Issue 50, *Titanic* (Final Issue), Spring 2012,
   accepted/publication coming.
   "Titanic at Belfast"

Westmeath Chronicle (Ireland) (1 poem, unverified)
   "Revenant"

POEMS PUBLISHED IN ANTHOLOGIES

Anderie Poetry Press Anthologies (3 poems, 2 verified)
   1994 *Songs of Glory* Anthology, p. 42.
      "Winter Gothic"
   1995 *How Do I Love Thee* Anthology, p. 103.
      "Sonas"
   1996 *Womankind: The Poetry of Women* Anthology
      "He Says"

Bergen Poets Anthologies (6 poems, all verified)
   30th Anniversary Anthology, 1999, pp. 12-13.
      "Flying into the Heartland," "Where Is My Father?"
   No. 13, 2000, pp. 28-29.
      "The Lions of Rome," "Rain"
   No. 14, 2002, pp. 30-31.
      "Aftermath," "Passage at Overpeck"
The Best of Feelings (1 poem, verified)
   1994, p. 25.
      "Miss Holybrooke in Central Park"

Friends for Life Poetry Anthology 2007 (2 poems, both verified)
   "Heartland," "Aftermath" (unpaginated anthology)

Lovelines — Poems of Love and Loss (4 poems, all verified)
   1995 - p. 6, 15, 28 & 31.
      "Dalkey," "Rained-Out Boulevard," "Shadow of a Rose,"
      "Where Is My Father?"

Main Street Poets & Writers Anthologies (32 poems, 31 verified)
   Vol. 1, 1998 (unverified at press time)
      "Tea Party"
         Vol. 4, 2000, pp. 18-21.

<306>

"After Rain," "Discretion," "Rain," "Sales Pitch"
"Blue Cover" edition, undated (likely 1999 or 2001), pp. 42-48.
  "Broken Blossoms," "Firs in Snow," "It Has to Do with Seeing,"
   "Just Like Jane," "Roan Inish."
Vol. 6, 2004, pp. 36-40.
  "Aftermath," "Autumn Rapture," "In Emily's Garden," "Mending
   Glass," "Poetry Class," "The Farm at Derry," "Three Rock
   Mountain"
Vol. 7, 2005, pp. 58-59.
  "Bird and the Sea," "In Ogdensburg," "Jersey Day,"
   "Passage at Overpeck"
Vol. 8, 2006
  "Alone in the Cemetery," "Brambles in Ireland," "Diner"
  (aka "At the Diner"), "Nice Day!", "Proper Manners,"
  "The Bike," "The Lions of Rome"
Vol. 9, 2007
  "Four Haiku," "The Paulinskill Valley Trail Sussex 6,"
   "The Secret" (aka "Ceircin"), "Upstate"

New Jersey Poetry Society, Inc. Anthologies (9 poems, all verified)
1995 Anthology
edge of sounds, pp. 6-9.
  "Brambles in Ireland," "Hearing Brodsky Read,"
   "Mending Glass," "Sonas," "The Holiness of Fall,"
   "The Source"
2003 Anthology
Road to Recovery, A Tribute to 9/11 and Other Poems, p. 57.
  "Aftermath" (First Place Winner, Spring/Summer 2002 contest)

2004 Anthology
"Seeds of April's Sowing" Poems, p. 1.
  "After Rain," "Shadow of a Rose"

<307>

PUBLISHED ARTICLES ON WRITERS (4, all verified)

Hamburger Anzeiger, October 11, 1954, p. 8.
　　　"In leicht singendem Tönfall: Ralph Ellison in Deutschland"
　　　Byline: Moira Fleischmann-Moore.

Feelings Poetry Journal, Fall 1996, pp. 7-8.
　　　"Out of Ireland: The Poetry of Seamus Heaney, Nobel
　　　　　Prize 1996"

Feelings Poetry Journal, Spring 1997, p. 4.
　　　"Joycevoice: The Poetry of James Joyce"

Feelings Poetry Journal, Vol. 8, No. 4, Summer/Fall 1997, pp. 12-13.
　　　"Heartbreak & Heroism: Anna Akhmatova"

OTHER PUBLISHED ARTICLES

Dalkey Community Council Newsletter
　　　September 1994, No. 191, pp. 5-6.
　　　"Memories of Dalkey"

<308>

POEM TITLES EXCLUDED
FROM THIS COMPILATION

"Trust," written pre-1989 — not located by press time.

"Lines to a Tom Cat," referred to as published in *Cats Magazine* in Florida — not located by press time.

"Poet" For David M. Written circa 1992-93 — not located by press time.

"Melody," "New Jersey, My State," "The Sound of Happiness" — need work.

"What Purpose Music," "On Opening a Map of Ireland," "New Windsor Settlement 1783" — incomplete fragments.

<309>

ABOUT THE EDITORS

DAVID MESSINEO, EDITOR is the publisher of *Sensations Magazine* (www.sensationsmag.com), a rare three-consecutive-year winner in the national American Literary Magazine Awards (including two First Place Awards, in 1994 and 1996). The author of six published poetry books, he has been an active fixture and influence in the New Jersey poetry scene since 1987, and a poetry editor since 1979. He was one of 26 individuals statewide to be honored with a 2009 New Jersey State Jefferson Award for Public Service for his research, publishing, and public programming efforts for both *Sensations Magazine* and its current parent company, The Six Centuries Club. He was a contributing editor to *A Funny Thing Happened on the Way to the Interview* by Gregory E. Farrell (Gillette, NJ: Edin Books, Inc., 1996), and one of five editors for *Beyond the Rift: Poets of the Palisades* (Providence, RI: The Poet's Press, 2010). David volunteered much of his spare personal time during 2010 to find, type, collect, and sequence this two-volume set of collected poems by Moira Bailis, in honor of their continuing writer/ editor relationship, and twenty years of their personal friendship. This is his first effort at compiling a sweeping, comprehensive "life's work" collection for an individual poet. In approaching this project, he took a light editing touch — changing spelling and punctuation as needed for consistency, assembling the missing stanza to the poem "Villanelle," and putting together the 2010 version of the poem "Courtesy," from Moira's multiple versions, in the "Variations on a Theme" section of *It Has To Do With Seeing*.

MELANIE A. PIMONT, ASSISTANT EDITOR is the former editor and publisher of *The North River Review* (1992-1998) and of *Lovelines: Poems of Love and Loss* (North River Press, 1995), where she was one of Moira's editors and poetry influences for close to a decade. Melanie was tasked with reconciling individual poems that had 20 to 30 variant texts, and creating a definitive new 2010 version of eight poems, which are published in the "Variations on a Theme" section of *It Has To Do With Seeing*.

<311>

ABOUT THIS BOOK

The body type for this book is ITC Cheltenham, a 1975 redesign by Tony Stan of an Oldstyle serif type originally designed in 1896 by Bertram Goodhue and Ingalls Kimball for The Cheltenham Press. Immensely popular through the 1920s and 1930s, the typeface is still used by *The New York Times*. In the early days of phototypesetting, Cheltenham was deprecated by many designers as a "hot metal" face associated with newspapers and "yellow journalism." Today, in its digital incarnations, the type design is appreciated for its visual charm and high legibility. Back matter and bibliographic material are set in Aldine, a face based on designs of the great humanist publisher and printer Aldus Manutius.

Block initials are a Poet's Press adaptation of an alphabet created for The Chiswick Press. Section titles are set in Morris Troy, a typeface designed by William Morris for the Kelmscott Press.

Typography and design for this book are by Brett Rutherford. The cover art includes a photograph by David Messineo. The portrait of Moira Bailis is a photograph by Stefan Bailis.

<312>

www.ingramcontent.com/pod-product-compliance
Lightning Source LLC
Chambersburg PA
CBHW022004080426
42733CB00007B/466